高等教育英语专业"十二五"规划教材

英语专业毕业论文写作指导

Thesis Writing Guide for English Majors

主　编	涂朝莲	程建山		
副主编	汪桂芬	王家芝	彭石玉	刘　珊
	冯　健	李玉梅	刘　沛	张媛媛
	陈　凯	田志远	陈　俊	
参　编	肖凤华	王丽丽	王婉华	杨　志
	王　伟	付小云	夏凌云	夏　芬
	向　霜	陈　萍	武艳霞	彭　红
	邓　妍	刘丽媛	沈蓉蓉	张由心

华中科技大学出版社
http://www.hustp.com
中国·武汉

图书在版编目(CIP)数据

英语专业毕业论文写作指导/涂朝莲,程建山主编. —武汉:华中科技大学出版社,2011.6(2023.8重印)
　ISBN 978-7-5609-6903-9

Ⅰ.英… Ⅱ.①涂… ②程… Ⅲ.英语-毕业论文-写作-高等学校-教材 Ⅳ.①G642.477 ②H315

中国版本图书馆 CIP 数据核字(2011)第 016874 号

英语专业毕业论文写作指导

涂朝莲　程建山　主编

策划编辑:彭中军
责任编辑:康　序
封面设计:龙文装帧
责任校对:李　琴
责任监印:张正林
出版发行:华中科技大学出版社(中国·武汉)　　电话:(027)81321913
　　　　　武汉市东湖新技术开发区华工科技园　　邮编:430223
录　　排:武汉兴明图文信息有限公司
印　　刷:武汉开心印印刷有限公司
开　　本:787mm×1092mm　1/16
印　　张:9.75
字　　数:260 千字
版　　次:2023 年 8 月第 1 版第 6 次印刷
定　　价:39.00 元

本书若有印装质量问题,请向出版社营销中心调换
全国免费服务热线:400-6679-118　　竭诚为您服务
版权所有　侵权必究

前　言

"英语专业毕业论文写作指导"是英语专业本科生的必修课。毕业论文(设计)是教学计划规定的综合性实践教学环节,能训练学生综合运用所学的基础知识、专业知识和基本技能,从而提高学生分析与解决实际问题的能力,使学生进行初步的科学研究训练,获得从事科学研究工作的初步能力,同时也是达到英语专业人才培养目标的一个重要环节。

根据《全国高等学校英语专业本科阶段教学大纲(2000)》,毕业论文是考查学生综合能力、评估学业成绩的一种重要方式。毕业论文用英语撰写,篇幅为 3 000～5 000 个单词,要求文字通顺、思路清晰、内容充实且有一定的独立见解。英语专业毕业论文写作既是对英语专业毕业生语言运用能力的考查,更是其创新能力的集中体现。

本书主要介绍英语专业毕业论文写作的要求和特点、学术论文的概念和分类,以及如何选题、收集整理资料、确定观点、拟订提纲、掌握论文格式和论证表达等八个重要环节,让学生既懂得毕业论文"是什么",又懂得具体操作时"怎么做"。

本书系统、详细地介绍了英语专业毕业论文各个部分的写作技巧和策略,包括论文选题、收集材料、开题报告、论文摘要、引言、文献综述、研究方法、研究结果及分析、结尾、致谢、注释、参考文献等。本书内容翔实、条理清晰、语言通俗易懂,具有很强的可读性及操作性。本书最大的亮点是增加了研究方法论这个章节,以第二语言研究为例,简介了学术论文写作中常用的研究方法和写作技巧,并列举了大量生动的实例,帮助学生更好地理解这些技巧与方法。

本书的实例均来自于湖北省各高校英语专业的优秀本科毕业论文,在此对这些论文的作者表示衷心的感谢。还要感谢华中科技大学出版社及时地出版此书,使得该书能这么快地与读者朋友们见面。另外,本书的出版得到了武汉工程大学"E＋"国家级人才培养模式创新实验区的资助,在此表示真诚的感谢!

相信本书一定会成为英语专业毕业生的良师益友,能在实践中帮助学生顺利完成毕业论文写作,圆满地毕业,走上更加辉煌的人生旅程。

由于编者水平有限,时间紧迫,书中疏漏之处在所难免,恳请使用本书的教师和学生不吝赐教,以便我们在修订时及时改正,以期更好地为广大师生服务。

编　者

2011 年 2 月

Contents

Chapter 1　Introduction ……………………………………………………… (1)
  1.1　Definition of the Graduate Thesis ……………………………………… (1)
  1.2　Major Features of the Graduate Thesis ………………………………… (2)
  1.3　Subject Areas for English Majors to Do the Research ………………… (3)
  1.4　Structure of the Graduate Thesis for English Majors ………………… (3)
    1.4.1　The Front Matter ………………………………………………… (3)
    1.4.2　The Text …………………………………………………………… (6)
    1.4.3　The Back Matter …………………………………………………… (8)

Chapter 2　Planning the Paper ……………………………………………… (10)
  2.1　Choosing a Topic ………………………………………………………… (10)
    2.1.1　Getting Start in Finding a Topic ………………………………… (10)
    2.1.2　The Principles of Choosing a Topic ……………………………… (12)
    2.1.3　How to Find an Appropriate Topic ……………………………… (13)
  2.2　Writing a Thesis Proposal ……………………………………………… (14)
    2.2.1　The Importance of Writing a Strong Thesis Proposal ………… (15)
    2.2.2　The Structure of a Thesis Proposal ……………………………… (15)
  2.3　Research Methodology …………………………………………………… (16)
    2.3.1　The Classification of Language Research ………………………… (16)
    2.3.2　Research Methods ………………………………………………… (17)
    2.3.3　Data Collection …………………………………………………… (21)
    2.3.4　Writing Techniques ……………………………………………… (23)

Chapter 3　Writing the Paper ……………………………………………… (32)
  3.1　Writing the Abstract of a Thesis ……………………………………… (32)
    3.1.1　What is an Abstract? ……………………………………………… (32)
    3.1.2　Structure of an Abstract ………………………………………… (32)
    3.1.3　Types of Abstract ………………………………………………… (33)
    3.1.4　How to Write a Good Abstract …………………………………… (34)
    3.1.5　The Extract of Key Words ………………………………………… (35)
  3.2　Writing the Introduction ………………………………………………… (35)
    3.2.1　The Major Elements in an Introduction ………………………… (36)
    3.2.2　Summary …………………………………………………………… (42)

3.3 Conclusion ……………………………………………………………… (42)
3.4 Revision …………………………………………………………………… (43)
3.5 Documentation …………………………………………………………… (48)
　　3.5.1 Format of Citation and Notes ……………………………………… (48)
　　3.5.2 Format of Works Cited …………………………………………… (54)
3.6 Acknowledgements ……………………………………………………… (60)
Chapter 4　Optional ………………………………………………………… (63)
4.1 A Thesis on English Education ………………………………………… (63)
4.2 A Thesis on Linguistics ………………………………………………… (84)
4.3 A Thesis on Translation ………………………………………………… (104)
4.4 A Thesis on Linguistics ………………………………………………… (124)
参考文献 …………………………………………………………………………… (149)

Chapter 1　　Introduction

According to *Syllabus for English Majors of Higher Education* in China, graduate thesis writing, as a means to assess students' comprehensive abilities and qualities, is an indispensable part of bachelor's degree education. The syllabus states explicitly that the thesis should be written in 3 000—5 000 English words with well-organized structure and substantial contents. In assessing the thesis, such factors are often considered, including the smoothness of language, the explicitness of the idea expressed, and the originality of the research method and conclusion.

Graduate thesis is different from those personal essays that students have written in their composition classes, in which they present their thoughts, feelings and opinions in English. Neither is it the assignment as a course paper that mainly consists of information gathered from books and encyclopedias. It is much more formal, involved and academic.

1.1　Definition of the Graduate Thesis

Graduate thesis is a kind of research paper that "should draw on original conclusion based on information derived from research"(Tian Guisen, 2006). Its main purpose is to inform the field experts about the author's new research findings or achievements, and to demonstrate the author's academic ability in the corresponding field as a partial requirement for a university degree.

Though research ability is a vital skill in thesis writing, it is such a common thing that it permeates our lives. We do some research when we investigate something such as a university, a course, a portable computer or even a tennis racket. For example, before we buy a certain brand of racket, we would usually check several stores to see what is in stock, how much it costs, what material it is made, its performance, and what level is its after-sales service like, etc. Besides, we would try to find how it feels like when playing it. After collecting all the information, we may still discuss it with our friends who know tennis racket well. It is not until we consider the price, the performance, the material and others' opinions that we make the final decision. So research usually involves three steps: to ask questions, to select the best way to find answers, and to interpret the findings in a reasonable way.

The research, in thesis writing, has to be systematic. It is the systematic application of scientific methods to the study of academic problems, or a systematic approach of finding answers to questions. The major research activities include identifying and choosing a research topic, gathering and reviewing previous research, assimilating others' findings and formulating one's own views, and then developing and expressing the ideas clearly and convincingly with supporting materials.

Everyone should possess essential research skills because almost every profession need them. Teachers do research to find out how their students can learn better. Restaurant managers do research to find out what their customers might like. As undergraduates, we should know how to solve a problem, how to make a decision or how to analyze the situation by seeking out relevant information, evaluating its usefulness, and combining it with our observation and experience to reach a conclusion. Whatever we plan to do after our graduation, knowing how to do research will be of great value to us. So writing graduate thesis is just the very opportunity for us to develop our research ability.

1.2 Major Features of the Graduate Thesis

A successful graduate thesis for the degree in English usually has the following features.

1. Academic

Though not so much advanced in research depth and scale, a B. A. degree graduate thesis is an academic scientific writing in that it has undergone a process of literature review, data exploration and analysis, and formulation of an independent view. It should be presented in a convincing and logical way, in an objective tone and supported with specific materials. In the thesis, students apply the theories, knowledge and skills that they have learned to the solution of specific problems.

2. Originality-oriented

Though a graduate thesis for a B. A. degree is usually not an original piece of work or an original contribution to a field, it is at least an original compilation, in which the author, using his independent interpretation and analysis, brings together pieces of information from different sources and combines them into a coherent whole to support the central statement. So it is an original combination of information, or originality-oriented.

3. Standard-governed

As a partial requirement for a B. A. degree, a graduate thesis should meet the standard and the specifications set by the university or college about its length, format, bibliography, binding sequence, etc.

4. Objective in tone

The graduate thesis should be written in an objective tone. In an academic writing, your tone and attitude should be serious and the style should be formal. Casual or oral expressions, are usually inappropriate, so they should be avoided in research paper. For example, first-person pronouns should be avoided, because they imply uncertainty, personal preference and individual taste.

5. No plagiarism

Plagiarism is to use someone else's words or ideas as your own without crediting the original writer. A graduate thesis forbids any kind of plagiarism. You may use and you are encouraged to use others' words or ideas but you must tell clearly in your paper where you take it.

1.3 Subject Areas for English Majors to Do the Research

A graduate thesis for English majors should be specialized in the study regarding English language, culture and literature or its comparison with Chinese.

Traditionally there are five broad subject areas for students to choose in their thesis writing: English literature, English linguistics, English language teaching and learning, English and Chinese translation, and English culture. In recent years, some foreign language schools offer quite a few job-oriented practical courses to English majors like international trade and business, international law, etc. So the study of English for specific purposes also wins the position to be an independent subject area in some universities.

These five or six broad subject areas can be developed into or narrowed down into many sub-areas and topics. For example, we can compare English literature with Chinese literature, or English culture with Chinese culture. And literature study can be narrowed down into the study of a specific literary work, a specific writer or certain literary genre etc. English linguistics also includes the study of English sounds, vocabulary, and syntax, etc. Culture is a very involved field, in which body language or etiquette can be chosen as the sub-topic. Anyway, students can choose certain area according to their individual interest and their tutor's instructions.

More detailed information about topics in each subject areas for the graduate thesis for English majors will be discussed in Chapter 2.

1.4 Structure of the Graduate Thesis for English Majors

The graduate thesis, as scholarly and academic writing, usually consists of three parts: the preliminaries (the front matter), the text (body) of the thesis, and reference materials (back matter). These parts can be further divided into subsections as follows.

(1) The front matter: cover page, title page, contents, abstract, (abstract in English, abstract in Chinese), acknowledgements, list of tables (if there are many tables), list of figures (if there are many figures).

(2) The text: introduction (literature review, methodology), the body, conclusion.

Or: introduction, literature review, methodology, result, discussion, and conclusion as recommended by the American Psychological Association.

(3) The back matter: bibliography, appendix (if there is).

The sequence presented above is not the actual writing sequence. A common practice is that the first matter is usually written last, the back matter second, and the text first. For the convenience of discussion, the sections are organized according to the actual sequence presented in a paper.

1.4.1 The Front Matter

Usually, the front matter of the graduate thesis includes the cover page, the title page, the table of contents, the abstract in English, the abstract in Chinese, acknowledgements. The following is the discussion of the cover page and the title page, and acknowledgements, and the other parts will be discussed later.

1. The cover page and the title page

Most universities and colleges have their own format of the cover page and the title page for theses. For an English thesis, the cover page usually includes information such as the English title of the thesis, the name, class, student number, major or orientation, instructor, the academic title of the instructor, and the school or college's name which the student is studying in and the date (usually includes the year and the month when the thesis is finished). The cover page is written in Chinese, although the title of the thesis should be written in English (See 4.1 for an example). The title page of a thesis should provide information such as the title of the thesis in English, the label of the thesis, the writer's name, the instructor's name and the academic title of the instructor, the signature of the writer and the date when the thesis is finished. Usually, there are some illustrative words that are centered below the title. The words are used to indicate that the thesis is submitted as a partial requirement for the student's undergraduate degree, such as "A thesis submitted to the faculty of ×× University in partial fulfillment of the requirements for bachelor's degree in English language and literature".

The title of the graduate thesis should be concise as well as descriptive and comprehensive. It should indicate the content of the thesis in order for the readers to have a general and clear idea about what is discussed in the thesis at the first sight. The title should also not be as good as specific as possible. For example, the title "An Analysis of the Image of Hester Prynne in *The Scarlet Letter*" "Hester Prynne's Purity in *The Scarlet Letter*". Because the latter focuses on only one point of Hester's image—purity, and omits the unnecessary phrase "An analysis of". Subtitles, if any, should delimit the subject described in the title. You can refer to Chapter 2 for more information about titles of the thesis.

The following are examples of thesis titles:

(1) The Child Image of The *Catcher in the Rye* from Linguistic Perspective;

(2) The Use of Zero Article Before Class Nouns;

(3) Factors of Martin Eden's Suicide;

(4) Factors Affecting Marriage in *Pride and Prejudice*;

(5) A Probe into Anti-Slavery of Mark Twain — From the Perspective of Jim in *The Adventures of Huckleberry Finn*;

(6) The Use of Body Language in English Teaching;

(7) Task-Based Language Teaching and Its Application in China;

(8) Various Circumstances That the Inversion Is Used Under the Comparison with Chinese;

(9) Individual Factors Contributing to Gatsby's Tragedy;

(10) The Direct Method and Its Application in Juvenile English Teaching;

(11) On Social Factors to the Failure of the American Dream—A Contrast Between Gatsby and Willy Loman;

(12) On the Psychological Development of Tom in *The Grapes of Wrath*;
(13) On the Study of the Teaching of Culture;
(14) Culture Conflicts in English Teaching;
(15) Cultural Differences of Chinese and English Color Words;
(16) Rhetoric in *Jane Eyre*;
(17) On the Causes of Tess's Tragedy;
(18) On Symbolism and Portraiture in *The Great Gatsby*;
(19) Multianalysis of "the Lost Generation" in *The Sun Also Rises*;
(20) On Robinson Crusoe's Character;
(21) The Use of Symbolism in *The Scarlet Letter*;
(22) On the Writing Features of *The Call of the Wild*;
(23) Character Analysis of Santiago in *The Old Man and The Sea*.

2. Acknowledgements

In acknowledgements, you thank those people who have given help to you in the process of your research and thesis writing. You usually give thanks to: ① your instructor; ② teachers or classmates who have once given you suggestions or advice on your research; ③ those who helped you to collect materials and data or do proof-reading; ④ those who gave you physical or mental support; ⑤ those who kindly permitted you to use their research instruments or materials, or those writers or researchers whose works you have cited or quoted.

Acknowledgements should be expressed specifically and sincerely. You should give your thanks to the specific people who have given you help, and state their specific contributions to your research or thesis writing. The statements of thanks should not be general and abstract. Being general or abstract makes people feel you are not sincere enough. You should tell what the person has done in relation to your research and thesis writing. Lastly, while you are expressing your thanks, you should not be over-modest. Being over-modest may lead the reader to conclude that you are an incompetent researcher, and as a result the reader may probably lose confidence in your argument. Look through and discuss the following examples of acknowledgements.

Example 1

I am deeply grateful to my instructor Mr. Cheng, for his wise encouragement and helpful suggestions throughout the entire period in which this paper was written. Without him, this paper would have never been fully completed. I have benefited considerably from his advice.

I also would like to thank the authors and publishers, whose articles and books my paper is based on.

Firstly, this acknowledgements is too general and abstract. It doesn't state the specific reasons for the writer's thanks to his instructor. Secondly, the language is not so sincere. It sounds like a formality rather than something from the bottom of his heart. Thirdly, this acknowledgements is not sufficient because the writer only thanks his instructor and some authors and publishers. As stated above, a number of people have offered their help to you in the process of research and writing, so you should express thanks to most of them, if not all.

> **Example 2**

Upon the fulfillment of this thesis, I would like to extend my gratitude to all those who have given me support and help to complete this thesis.

First and foremost, my special gratitude goes to Professor Zhang Yuanyuan, my respectable instructor. She has ever been patient and professional in giving me guidance and instructions, during the period of thesis preparing and writing. Her valuable suggestions and insights have proved less possible errors in my thesis. Without her profound knowledge, constant encouragement and patient help, this thesis would have been impossible.

I am also grateful to my classmates and friends whom I have consulted so frequently. They have given me numerous valuable suggestions on this thesis.

Finally, I would express my deep gratitude to my family whose love, care and encouragement made it possible for me to complete the present thesis.

This acknowledgements is written clearly, specifically, and sincerely. The writer thanks mainly his instructor with specific reasons and sincere language. He also expresses his thanks to his classmates and friends, and his family for their help and support. The whole acknowledgements sounds smooth and vivid.

1.4.2 The Text

Generally speaking, every essay or paper is made up of three parts: introduction, body and conclusion. However, a graduate thesis is much longer and more complex than an essay or a term paper. It is often divided into smaller parts such as introduction, literature review, methodology, result, discussion, and conclusion. Here we just introduce each of them briefly, for more details you can refer to the next chapters.

1. Introduction

Introduction is the first part of the text, which usually contains background information and the thesis statement.

A good way to begin a thesis is to provide general background information on the subject. By providing background material you make the reader aware of the context surrounding the topic. You may begin with a discussion of past research related to the particular investigation, through which you make the reader familiar with your research and show how your research is related to preceding researches.

The thesis statement tells the reader in brief that what research you are going to do in the body of your thesis. It directs the reader's attention to your major points and the purpose of your thesis. It is often the last paragraph of the introduction. The following are some examples.

This paper compares and analyzes the causes of western culture invasion and attempts to figure out the proper measures that should be taken to deal with this situation.

This paper makes a comparison of these two novels (Pride and Prejudice and Little Women), attempting to expose different personalities connected with family education and social background, which maybe give some instructions on children's education.

2. The body

The body is the most important and longest section of your thesis, which usually consists of a number of chapters. If your research involves certain experiment, as recommended by the American Psychological Association, the body should consist of literature review, methodology, results and discussion chapters.

Literature review may be a free-standing part. It commonly serves for a subsequent chapter or section that presents the author's own research or analysis. It is a critical view of the existing research that is significant to the work you are carrying out. You first need to read as many as possible researches at home and abroad that are related to your own research and evaluate these researches. However, in writing the literature review, you should focus on only several important researches that are most closely related to your own research. The most important thing is that you should evaluate these researches by pointing out their advantages and defects, and their relationships to your own research. In literature review, you can find a sound basis for the significance or value of your own research. These researches conducted by previous researchers may serve as the background information or theories for your research.

The methodology chapter, if there is any, describes the design of the study. It includes general as well as specific research questions or hypotheses, information about subjects, instruments, the procedures for data collection and data analysis. The information presented in this chapter should be explicit and transparent so that other researchers can get to know the whole process of your research and they can replicate your experiment if they want.

The results and discussion chapter is a report of the research findings, which provide answers to your research questions. While the results section usually include some scores and statistics, the discussion section is an interpretation of the results in which you explain the possible reasons for a specific finding, the significance of the findings, and the link between the present findings and the previous ones. The discussion may go along with each finding presented or it may be an independent chapter from the results.

In the body of the thesis, your ideas should be developed in detail. You should prove your points of view by using specific and sufficient examples and quotations from other writers or researchers, and use transitional words to ensure a smooth flow of ideas from one paragraph to another.

3. Conclusion

The conclusion of a thesis usually summarizes the main points, and points out the implications of the research.

The conclusion part can help the readers to put all the parts together, to see things all at once. It restates the thesis statement, reviews the research process, and sums up the research results. It may point out the relationships between each part and their significance. Here is an example.

Euphemism appears with false appearance, and exerts a subtle influence on exposing the truth. Euphemism is to use the neutral or pleasant words to express some awkward or offensive contents. The positive functions of euphemism are to coordinate interpersonal relationships, release the contradictions and avoid conflicts. The negative functions are to confound right with wrong, beautify the shameful behaviors and conceal the essence. Language itself has no class, but different people, political parties and countries can consider it a tool to serve their purposes. This is why euphemisms are called "comfortable words", or "cosmetic words". In daily life, we should pay attention to the influences that the positive and negative functions of euphemism bring us, and keep the negative functions from corrupting our thoughts.

The above example sums up the definition of euphemism and the positive and negative functions of euphemism, and conclude that we should keep its negative functions from corrupting out thoughts. By the conclusion, the reader can easily know the main purpose of the thesis.

Another way to conclude a thesis is to consider the implications of the points you have discussed in the thesis. That is to point out the theoretical or practical value of the research, and its instructive meaning to the society. Here is an example.

To sum up, the awareness of the importance of home tutorials is essential for its success. We need to explore the problems and find the reasons lying these problems in order to find out appropriate methods in tutorial and lay a good foundation for children's success. The following are two rules this paper wants to tell parents: firstly, pay more attention to educate children how to be oneself, which means when children are young, parents should inculcate them with a sense of integrity and responsibility for individual, society and the nation. In this regard, parents should set good examples. Secondly, apply harmonious, understanding teaching method, which help to shorten the distance and arouse resonance with children, just as the Marches do.

The conclusion firstly emphasizes the importance of home tutorials of parents to children and then gives two pieces of advice for parents on how to educate their children well. After reading the conclusion part, the reader can get some implications about how to use appropriate ways to educate their children.

1.4.3　The Back Matter

The back matter contains two sections: bibliography and appendices. They are important materials for a thesis but are not to be integrated into the body of a thesis because they may disrupt the smooth flow of the text.

1. Bibliography

A bibliography is a list of the sources you have used to get information for your paper. In MLA(Modern Language Association) style, it comes under the heading of Works Cited; in APA(American Psychological Association) style, it is called References. Reference lists, works cited lists, and bibliographies are similar, but not actually the same. References and works cited pages will contain only the works you actually cite in your paper—even if you have read many sources to become informed about your topic, while in a bibliography page you list all of the sources you have consulted to become informed about your topic (in contrast to listing only the sources you actually cite).

You will find it easier to prepare your final bibliography if you keep record of each book, encyclopedia, articles, or journals while you are reading and taking notes. When you refer to any of these sources, you'd better write down the full title, author, place of publication, publisher, and the date of publication for each source. When assembling a final bibliography, list your sources (books, texts, articles, internet sources, etc.) in alphabetical order by the author's last name. Sources that do not have authors (encyclopedia, articles) should be alphabetized by title. There are different styles and formats for bibliographies, use the one your university suggests.

Nowadays universities often require students to write their bibliographies in the way references and works cited are written. A common problem in students' papers is that the bibliography includes the works that are not cited in the text while the cited works are excluded. This is due to the lack of timely revision of the references along with repeated revisions of the text. A solution to this problem is to go through the whole paper and tick the references in the bibliography that appear in the text, delete those that have not been cited, and add cited works to the bibliography if they are not quoted in the thesis.

2. Appendices

An appendix, although by no means an essential part of every thesis, is a useful way to list materials related to the text but not suitable for the inclusion in it. Appendices may include tables too detailed for text presentation, too many illustrations to be included in the text, technical notes on method, schedules and forms used in collecting materials, copies of documents not generally available to the reader, case studies too long to be put into the text, and sometimes figures or other illustrative materials.

All appendices go at the end of a thesis, never at the end of the chapters to which they may pertain. Materials of different categories should be placed in separate appendices. When there is more than one appendix, each should be given a number of a letter such as Appendix 1, 2,... or Appendix One, Two, ... or Appendix A, B,....

Chapter 2   Planning the Paper

2.1   Choosing a Topic

Choosing a topic for your graduate thesis is probably the most important and difficult part of the whole thesis writing. It is important because it decides all the following process, i. e. what data to explore and collect, what thesis statement to formulate, what conclusion to make, etc. It is difficult because it involves a lot of laborious work like identifying a general subject area, defining the topic and narrowing down it, and stating the proposition as a question.

Most universities offer a list of possible topics for students to refer to or to choose from. Sometimes the instructors specify a broad area of study, or give students a free choice of topics within a broad range according to their own research field. Anyway, the early the students begin to choose topics for their paper, the better it is.

2.1.1   Getting Start in Finding a Topic

Whether you have to choose a topic of your own or from a list of possible topics in a broad range, you will find the following ways helpful to start with.

1. Choosing a topic that interests you

You are encouraged to choose a topic that you are genuinely interested in. With real interests in the topic, you will be more willing to spend time researching. The following questions may help you to make a decision.

(1) What subject(s) are you interested in?

(2) What interests you most about a particular subject?

(3) Is there anything you are puzzled about with regard to that subject?

2. Consulting other people

In choosing a topic to write, you can consult many people. But first of all, consult your instructor. Your instructor is usually the specialist in the field who knows well about the general development of the field, the trend, the problems to be solved, and the research focus. Talking with your instructor can save you a lot of time exploring materials, and find something interesting and worthwhile.

Besides, you can also talk with your classmates, friends, those who have just graduated, or post graduates. Their experience and ideas will be very helpful for your in making decision.

3. Exploring library resources for a topic

Either when you don't know what topic to write about or when you are not sure whether you want to pursue a topic, you can turn to library for more information, where you can find excellent sources either in paper form or in electronic form, such as periodicals, book index, encyclopedia, biographical dictionaries, computer databases, etc.

(1) Periodicals.

Periodicals — journals, magazines and newspapers — are published frequently. So they can provide you more current information and opinions, undiscussed area of inquiry or unresolved controversies in their own work. But you have to know that this kind of topic is usually very challenging for an undergraduate to choose in his/her graduate thesis.

Periodical indexes categorize almost all periodical articles. The most famous of such indexes include *Readers' Guide to Periodical Literature*, *Humanities Index*, *Social Sciences Index*, and *MLA international Bibliography*. Those categories of articles not only give you a clear picture of the current research trends and focuses in a certain field, but also provide information about what work has been already done so that you can avoid in your writing. A brief look at those categories, titles of the articles and the key words might trigger ideas for a topic.

(2) Books index.

A book index, usually located at the end of a book, lists alphabetically the book's major contents, topics, subtopics, ideas, names of the person and place mentioned. It is also very useful in discovering specific topics.

(3) Encyclopedia.

Encyclopedia covers practically all subjects, with its entries often alphabetically arranged. Articles in encyclopedia are often authoritative summaries and discussions written by carefully chosen experts in the related fields. Though most of the articles in it do not provide in-depth information, it serves as a place to start and you may find a topic you are interested in. Besides, it suggests related bibliography that leads to valuable sources.

(4) Biographical dictionaries.

For a graduate thesis for English majors, famous men of letters and translators and literary works are always good topics. Before you use these sources, consider whether you need a volume of famous people who are living or dead, so that you can find a more useful biography.

(5) Computer databases.

Most university libraries now subscribe to online database networks and own CD-ROM machines that are accessed through the library's computer terminals. Most research databases are electronic indexes listing thousands of books and articles.

4. Internet resources

Now university students rely more on internet resources for information. Online resources are especially helpful for finding a topic. When looking for a topic, students may surf on the internet for related topics, articles and books that might trigger an idea for the topic.

5. Brainstorming

Brainstorming is a way of finding and developing a proper topic by listing relevant words and phrases in rapid succession. We can sit down and write down all the thoughts and ideas on the topic that come to our mind, no matter how simple or obvious they might seem. Don't worry about what idea comes first or how to group them. These ideas and thoughts may look like a junk, but after sorting and grouping, they may provide valuable ideas for a topic. Fig. 2-1 illustrates a brainstorming process with the topic of sonnets.

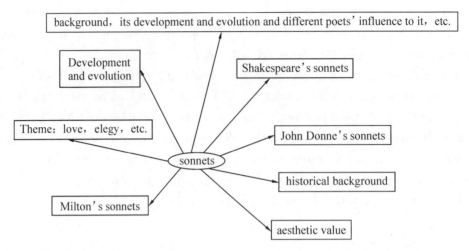

Fig. 2-1　Illustrates a brainstorming process with the topic of sonnets

2.1.2　The Principles of Choosing a Topic

When you are trying to decide on a topic, the following principles are good for you to make the right decision.

1. Choosing a topic of considerable importance to your reader

The topic should promise you and the reader real value and significance. Instructors at colleges and universities who assign the paper are usually the primary and immediate readers. There are other potential readers as well. When planning your paper, you should keep in mind that the reader is well informed and knowledgeable about the subject, yet needs to know more.

Of course, the most important thing is subjective judgments. A topic that may seem trivial to persons who specialized in one field holds great significance for researchers in another. You can consult your instructor about the significance of your topic and your paper can convince readers of its significance.

2. Choosing a topic of appropriate scope

The topic you choose should neither be too broad nor too narrow. Many graduate theses are unsuccessful because they cover too many fields. They are too general in scope to make deep and insightful research treatment. So restrict your general subject area until you arrive at something that you can explore in detail. Of course, if a topic is too narrow or too small, there is hardly any room for you to develop it into an interesting research paper with certain page requirements.

3. Choosing a topic of manageability

A topic for graduate thesis should be the one you are familiar with. It is better that you have taken some courses related with the topic in your college study. And a topic, interesting and worthwhile as it is, may not be suitable if you can not find enough data necessary for the research. As your thesis should be written in English, more than half of your data should be in English so that the quality of your language could be guaranteed. The resources of the libraries of your university or of the city you are living, as well as your access to electronic materials, should help guide your choice of topic.

2.1.3 How to Find an Appropriate Topic

1. Narrowing down your topic

As discussed above, many graduate theses are unsuccessful because they are too general. Then how to find a topic of appropriate scope? When you have chosen a broad area to write about, first of all, you had better go to library or read an introductory book about the subject area to broaden your knowledge. Then you are more likely to choose a proper topic for the research.

Suppose you feel interested in Chinese and English translation and would like to write something about it. After exploring library resources, you realize translation is a very broad area and can be studied from different perspectives: studies of translation theories, studies of translation methods, different text genres and their translation, special uses of language and their translation, factors affecting translation, etc. You can not cover them all. You need to make further decision and choose one perspective in your thesis. You may choose to write about specific uses of language and their translation. This includes those subjects like: idioms translation, slang translation, rhetoric devices translation, proper names translation, advertisement translation, news translation, legal language translation, financial English translation, etc. If you investigate further, you can still narrow down the topics above. For example, if you choose to write about news translation, you can study the English translation of Chinese neology in news, Chinese translation of English news titles, cultural factors in news translation, etc.

2. Formulate a thesis statement

After you have chosen a topic, you will read more and narrow down the topic so as to focus it into a question and turn your question into a thesis statement. Topic is a relatively broad area of interest, but the word question indicates a particular part or aspect of a topic that is narrow enough to investigate and write about. For instance, news translation is a topic, and the cultural factors influencing news translation is a question. Thesis statement is the theme in a research paper. It means an assumption about your topic, an approach to it, attitude towards it, or a proposition to be examined. It is the controlling idea that determines what kind of material you will look for.

A thesis statement is usually a single sentence which summarizes the fundamental argument of the thesis paragraph. If your idea seems complex or your paper is long and involved, you may need more than one sentence to present your thesis. Typically, the thesis statement will appear near the end of the introductory paragraph, letting readers know what will be discussed. Generally speaking, we don't always have a finished thesis when we begin to write, but we should establish a tentative working thesis early on in our writing process.

In spite of the fact that it will probably change, a working thesis is important for two reasons: ① it focuses your thinking, research, and investigation on a particular point about the topic and keeps you on track; ② it provides concrete questions to ask about purpose, readers, and your stance and tone.

A working thesis usually has two parts: a topic part and a comment part. The topic part states the topic. The comment part makes an important assumption or claim about the topic. The controlling idea of the comment part determines the design of the graduate thesis and ensures that the topic is manageable.

Here are some examples of theses developing from different topics.

Example 1

Topic   Advertisement language study

Question   How does advertisement language help promote sales?

Thesis statement   Advertisement language <u>makes full use of the seven types of meanings advocated by Leech</u> to affect its audience so as to promote sales of the product it advertised.

Example 2

Topic   Literary work translation

Question   How can a translator affect the reproduction of aesthetic effects in literary translation?

Thesis statement   In the reproduction of aesthetic effects of a literary work a translator plays a crucial role <u>in three aspects: perceptivity, comprehension and imagination capacity</u>.

Example 3

Topic   The use of textbooks in language classrooms

Question   How does the use of textbooks in language classrooms affect English language teaching?

Thesis statement   Although textbooks play a central role in English language teaching, there are <u>crucial differences in the ways in which textbooks are creatively used</u>.

Sometimes a thesis statement is more than one sentence. Here is an example.

The purpose of this paper is to examine various aspects of transportation in the United States. The subject may be logically divided <u>*into several categories: the private automobile, alternatives to the private automobile, the feasibility of implementing those alternatives, and the economic and social implications of adopting them*</u>*.*

In the above examples, the thesis statement contains a topic, a comment about the topic. And the comment part is usually written with a controlling idea (underlined in those examples) to narrow down the topic further and ensures that it will be manageable.

It is often difficult to compose a thesis statement. You will probably need to revise several versions, juggle phrases and search for more specific words until you have a sentence that clearly expresses your topic and controlling idea. This tentative working thesis is always subject to revision until you have completed writing. In short, an effective thesis statement should be specific, arguable and explicit and direct.

2.2 Writing a Thesis Proposal

A thesis proposal is a kind of research proposal — a document presenting a general overview of your research work. It is generally done as a written report and presented on a seminar. A committee of supervisors or instructors is to analyze your report and to give its impersonal, objective judgment whether the research project is feasible. So only after it is done and approved by the committee can you start your draft writing of the graduate thesis.

A thesis proposal is not always a necessary part for thesis writing. But some universities or colleges do have the requirement of it.

2.2.1　The Importance of Writing a Strong Thesis Proposal

A thesis proposal is useful for the thesis writing for the following reasons.

(1) The thesis proposal clearly defines a research problem or question, which is central to the success of a research project. It helps you to determine whether your project is doable before you begin writing the thesis.

(2) If you take time to clearly describe your project in your proposal, you will be able to write your thesis faster and more easily because you have solidified key elements.

(3) The thesis proposal can be used as a guide to help you keep on track while writing your thesis.

Once you have been asked to submit a thesis proposal you should clearly realize that its goal is to convince a thesis supervisor or thesis committee that the research project is feasible, which it means as follows.

(1) Your research is significant and worthwhile.

(2) You know how to approach and execute the project.

(3) Your research corresponds to your knowledge and interest.

(4) It can be completed within the time required.

2.2.2　The Structure of a Thesis Proposal

Usually your university or college has a clear format about what the thesis proposal should be like if it is required as a part of your graduate thesis files. But most proposals have the following elements in order:

(1) Title of the research;

(2) Introduction—it involves the reader in reading your proposals and sets the framework for your proposed projects about its significance, your motivation, the background information home and abroad;

(3) Literature review—a brief but exact description of the sources for your research, outlining their significance for the work;

(4) Key questions—the main questions of your research;

(5) Approaches/methods—the methods you have chosen to use in order to ensure the validity and accuracy of the results;

(6) Work plan including time table;

(7) Conclusions and implications of your research—explain the results expected, your work's achievements' contribution to the field;

(8) Initial list of references.

Here is a sample of thesis proposal of a university. If a university has a fixed format of thesis proposal for its all graduates, it is always be written in Chinese. Table 2-1 is "××届毕业论文开题报告".

Table 2-1 ××届毕业论文开题报告

学生姓名		专业/班级	
毕业设计(论文)题目			
指导教师姓名		职称	
一、课题背景			
二、毕业论文研究的问题及研究方案			
三、毕业论文预期成果及创新			
四、主要参考文献			
教研室(学科部)审核意见 教研室(学科部)主任(签字)_____ 年 月 日			
学院审核意见 主管院长(系主任)签字_____ 年 月 日			

注:此表中的一、二、三、四项,由学生在教师的指导下填写。

2.3　Research Methodology

2.3.1　The Classification of Language Research

　　Generally speaking, scientific research is divided into basic research and applied research. While in foreign language research, this kind of division is helpful because foreign language research involves many aspects and subjects ranging from the establishment and application of research models to the application of all kinds of results or findings to classroom teaching and learning.

Generally the research of theoretical models belongs to basic research. For example, Grice found that there must be some mechanics guiding people's daily conversations. There are must always a purpose or common topic for people's talk, and they must be willing to cooperate with each other. Later he generalized this mechanism as Cooperative Principle. Applied research discusses the application of the research model. After proposing the research model, the researchers should testify the model in practice. For instance, after Grice put forward the famous Cooperative Principle, many researchers testified this theory and found many defects of it, which led to several different but similar principles.

Practical research puts scientific results or findings into practical language teaching and learning. With the development of linguistic theories, a lot of them have been used in language teaching and learning. For example, during the 1970s, influenced by American structuralist linguistic view, structuralist syllabus dominated English teaching. After the introduction of communicative competence and systematic-functional grammar, communicative syllabus and notion-functional syllabus are rather popular in English teaching.

The above interpretation shows that the distinctions between these three kinds of research are not so clear-cut, and actually they influence each other and depend on each other. Basic research directs applied and practical research; in many cases, applied research and practical research directly influence the modification and perfection of theories found in basic research.

2.3.2 Research Methods

1. Synthetic approach and analytic approach

Just like other things in the world, foreign language teaching and learning is a complex thing, involving many different elements. Researchers may choose any of them to conduct research. For example, they can research the influence of the first language on the second language acquisition, or the impact of learners' personality to the second language acquisition rate, or the effect of social environment on acquisition and the interactive effects of men and social environment, or the psychological or biological basis of language acquisition. We can hardly exhaust the research aspects or fields. However, we can divide them into different categories according to their common features of these factors, such as biological factor, language factor, affective factor, and social factor, etc. Each category is a sub-system of language learning and each sub-system includes many sub-divisions. For example, language system can be divided into phonetics, phonology, morphology, syntax, semantics, pragmatics, etc. Each system can be divided into smaller sub-systems. These sub-systems are not independent from one another. Instead they are interrelated. It is hard to imagine one only learns vocabulary but no grammar or only grammar without learning vocabulary; likewise, one can't learn only language forms without learning language use.

To study such a complex field, there are two approaches to choose. One is to begin from the whole thing or a larger sub-system in order to investigate the relationships between the elements. The other is to begin from the smallest elements. After researching these smallest elements thoroughly, then we put these sub-systems together into larger systems and finally we can investigate the relationships of the whole. The first approach is called synthetic approach and the second analytic approach. Synthetic approach is similar to holistic perspective and analytic approach is close to constituent perspective. Holistic perspective views each sub-system as an interrelated whole while constituent perspective studies a group of individual factors and then put them together into a sub-system. These two approaches have their own advantages and they are not contradictory but dependent on each other.

For example, language level is an abstract concept. If we use the achievement of a comprehensive test including listening, translation, cloze, reading comprehension and writing to show a student's language level, it is a holistic view. If we divide language level into phonetics, intonation, vocabulary, grammar, reading comprehension, etc., it is a constituent view. In most cases, we can adopt the two approaches simultaneously. The results of the two approaches can be complementary to each other, thus making the research result more accurate.

2. Heuristic approach and deductive approach

The distinctions between heuristic approach and deductive approach lie in the objectives of the research. The objective of a heuristic approach is to describe what happens or to gather data and generate hypotheses about the phenomena studied. However, in deductive approach, the aim is to test hypotheses in order to develop a theory about the phenomena in question.

If the aim of the research is heuristic, the investigators observe and record some aspects or context of second language. There may no complete theories or models to guide the researcher or to stimulate research specific questions at this point. Data are collected in an attempt to include as much of the contextual information as possible. These data may then be categorized or analyzed or written up descriptively. Often the result of such research may be the formulations of hypotheses.

For example, there was a study which tried to find out why some second language learners are more successful than others. It is decided to observe language learners in classroom environments and to record as much information as possible about the learning process in that context. The aim is to observe as many factors as possible which may be related to successful second language acquisition (learners' raising hands to participate, writing in notebooks, talking to themselves and to their peers, etc.).

We may have some general ideas, based on the work of other researchers as to why some learners achieve more than others. We may nonetheless choose to approach the question with as few preconceptions as possible. In the process of analyzing the data, we may find ourselves with lists of a great many observed behaviors. We may then decide to look at all of the different behaviors and try to categorize them into different patterns. For example, our observations may reveal that verbal and non-verbal behavior should be considered as separate categories. The verbal interactions of teachers with learners may also reveal patterns which are different from those among the learners.

Note that when the aim of the research is heuristic, an effort is made to avoid preconceptions about what good language learners do. We describe, analyze and explain the actual behavior or unprocessed observations in order to find the patterns which are suggested by the data themselves. This process is considered to be heuristic because of its inductive nature. A heuristic objective enables us to discover patterns, behaviors, explanations and to form questions or actual hypotheses for further research.

In deductive or hypothesis-testing approach, the investigators may begin with hypotheses which are based on observations suggested by heuristic research. The deductive approach, distinct from the heuristic approach, begins with a preconceived notion or expectation about the second language phenomena to be investigated. In this sense, it may be said that deductive research is hypothesis-driven. That is, the research begins with a question or a theory which narrows the focus of the research and allows the second language phenomena to be investigated systematically.

For instance, in cognitive psychology, notions of "field independence" and "field dependence" have been developed. This theoretical construct claims that some subjects are able to perceive a geometric figure embedded in a background pattern while others can not. Subjects can be categorized as either dependent on the field or background upon which the pattern appears (field dependent) or independent of that field or background (field independent). This construct is regarded as a characteristic of learning style.

The first thing to notice from the example is that we begin with a possible idea about how to categorize learners and we begin with an assumption or hypothesis that this categorization may apply to second language learning as well. If we apply this concept to second language learning, we may hypothesize that good language learners may be "field independent". These students can extract language rules from the language data in which the rules are embedded. Poor language learners are "field dependent", which would explain their difficulty in learning a language from natural language data. The concept of "field dependence" can thus become the source of hypotheses about second language acquisition. The differences between heuristic approach and deductive approach are shown in the following Table 2-2.

Table 2-2 The differences between heuristic approach and deductive approach

Heuristic	Deductive
Data-driven	Hypothesis-driven
No preconceptions	Makes predictions
Can generate hypotheses	Tests hypotheses
Product: description or hypotheses	Product: theory

3. Qualitative and Quantitative Approaches

Punch(1998:4) thinks that both qualitative and quantitative research are both empirical research but their data are different. The data of quantitative research are numbers but the data of qualitative research are not. Certainly this distinction is too simplified. Let's consider the following two examples.

Example 1

You want to know the vocabulary of students and then you design a research test. You take 100 words at random from the syllabus and require students to give their Chinese meanings. The total score is 100, each vocabulary one point, so the total score got by each

student shows their vocabulary.

> **Example 2**

The research attempts to investigate whether students with higher level of second language use different reading strategies compared with students whose level of second language is lower. There are 4 research subjects, who are undergraduates majoring in Japanese and Russian, and English is their second foreign language. They are excellent students in their majors but in English learning, 2 of them are in upper intermediate level and the other 2 are in lower intermediate level. The researcher chooses 2 English passages which are suitable to their reading level. Each student is required to tell what they are thinking while reading. The whole process is recorded and transcribed into words. Then the researcher classify and introduce these students' use of reading strategies. Finally, the researcher compares how the two groups of students use reading strategies (Lu, 1997).

From the above two examples, we can find that quantitative data are mostly numbers while qualitative data are mostly words and descriptions. For instance, if you want to investigate the strategies used by students to enlarge their vocabulary, you can make interviews with 20 students and ask them to describe how they enlarge their vocabulary. This is a question without a definite answer, so these students must give different answers. If we record students' answers sentence by sentence, the data collected are words and descriptions.

Besides the difference in data, there are other distinctions between quantitative research and qualitative research. Malhotra thinks that the research objectives of them are different. The objective of the former is to investigate the known and established variables and the hypotheses about these variables; the objective of the latter is to establish variables that need further study and formulate hypotheses that can be tested in further studies. In other words, quantitative research is mostly used to test previous research results but qualitative research is mostly used in exploratory research.

The research question of quantitative research is specific and clear, and presented before the data are collected. The research question in qualitative research is usually broad but with the progress of research the research question is focused gradually. So in qualitative research, the focuses of data collection are constantly changing.

Quantitative research needs large samples to satisfy the need of statistics, but qualitative research may only cover small samples because qualitative research takes more time and effort, and a large sample is usually beyond the researcher's ability. The procedure of data collection of quantitative research is fixed and rigid while it is flexible for qualitative research and it can be adjusted in some cases.

Quantitative data can only be analyzed statistically, but qualitative data can choose either qualitative analysis or quantitative analysis.

Because qualitative research is mostly used in exploratory research and involves fewer number of cases, so the result of qualitative research is less extensively used as quantitative research. Table 2-3 clearly shows the distinctions between quantitative research and qualitative research.

Table 2-3 The distinctions between quantitative research and qualitative research

—	Quantitative Research	Qualitative Research
Objective	Test definite variables; hypothesis-testing	Make clear variables; hypothesis-making
Question	Clear before data collection	Becoming specific in the process of research
Samples	Big samples	Small samples
Data collection	Fixed procedure and structure	Flexible and dynamic procedure and structure
Data analysis	Statistical analysis	Mostly qualitative analysis, also use statistical analysis
Result	Extensively used	Lack extensive use

2.3.3 Data Collection

1. What Are Data

Data may include all behaviors observable by the researcher in a second language event such as a language lesson, sentences of a specific type that learners utter, or subjects' opinions about speakers of the second language. Second language research data can be drawn from any of the behaviors involved in a second language teaching or learning event. They may cover a wide variety of phenomena such as learner utterance, conversations, strategies used for producing and solving language problems, attitudes towards learning a language and towards its speakers, language used by teacher and students in classroom lessons, performances of learners on language skills such as reading, writing, translation, and so on.

However, determining what constitute data in a second language research depends primarily on the purpose of the study and on the specific variables to be identified. Thus the first step in the process is to find out the variables of the study, that is, identify specific behaviors which can provide acceptable evidence for describing them.

For example, if you want to carry out a research project in which the variable "language proficiency" needs to be investigated, the first step is to identify the relevant data which can define "language proficiency". These data may be specific behaviors such as ability to pronounce words correctly, and to speak the language with a certain degree of fluency, possession of certain vocabulary, use of an appropriate register in a conversation with native speakers, mastery of specific grammatical structures, and so on. Any of these behaviors will be considered as the data of the study, since each provides an indication of language proficiency.

2. Means of Collecting Data

Once the researcher has decided what data to collect, the next step is to decide how to collect them. In this regard, the researcher will have to select the appropriate data collection procedures from a large pool of available procedures.

If one of the data that show "language proficiency" is "ability to pronounce words accurately", the researcher may collect data through a test where the subject is required to pronounce words while being recorded in a language lab. If the researcher wants to collect data of the subject's pronunciation in a natural conversation, the subject's pronunciation in that natural setting may be observed and recorded. In addition to the two procedures just mentioned, other data collection procedures such as questionnaire or interviews can be used as well. It is also possible, at times, to use multiple procedures in one study and thus to obtain data from a variety of sources.

In qualitative types of research (heuristic/synthetic), where a phenomenon is studied within a natural context, data are often collected by several means, with one piece of data leading to the next. For example, a researcher is interested in finding out how a number of immigrants acquire the language of the country they live in, she interviews a number of learners and asks them to report on their experiences and to reflect on the processes that they learn the language. She also observes the immigrants using the language as they interact with colleagues at work and with spouses and children at home. In addition, she reviews records which include letters they write in the target language, notes and reports they write at work, as well as their grades and papers in the language classes they are enrolled. She also reviews diaries of the learners which describe the process and problems of learning the language and some experiences he or she had as an immigrant in the first few months of arriving in the new country.

In the above example, the researcher uses a variety of data collection procedures for collecting data about the process of second language learning by immigrants. By using a variety of procedures and by obtaining data from a variety of sources, the researcher often obtains rich and comprehensive data. Such data usually provide an expanded and global picture of the phenomenon that cannot be obtained by data from a single source, as each source provides additional data. The following is a brief list of some collection methods.

(1) Interviews. A variety of interview types are used in second language research. However, in qualitative research, the most typical interviews are those which are open, informal, and unstructured. The researcher may give a lot of directions to subjects who will respond to certain questions, but he should try to avoid making the subjects conscious of the fact that they are taking part in a research study.

(2) Open observations. Observations are very common in qualitative research, in which the research usually observes a number of behaviors taking place simultaneously. The observation is performed either by a participant observer who becomes an integral part of the observed situation, or by a non-participant observer who records in detail as an outsider, all the behaviors that take place.

(3) Record reviews. This, another commonly used procedure in qualitative research, involves collecting data from documents and other materials. The content of these data is reviewed and analyzed by a process called content analysis. Examples of such records and documents are records of meetings, report cards, letters, notebooks, historical records, documents, correspondence, tests, papers, and teacher's comments.

(4) Diaries. The subjects or the researcher record in writing, different aspects of a process or a phenomenon. Diaries have been used in a number of second language studies, especially to collect data on subjects' experiences as students.

2.3.4 Writing Techniques

The most commonly used writing techniques in thesis writing are cause-and-effect, division-and-classification, comparison-and-contrast, exemplification and definition. Some researches are conducted to investigate the causes or reasons of some behaviors or phenomena.

1. Cause-and-Effect

When writing a cause-and-effect essay, we discuss the reasons for something, and then discuss the result of it. Sometimes we emphasize the causes while at other times we emphasize the effects. It depends on the objective and subject matter of the thesis. We may start with a situation (the effect) and then search for causes in the past. We may begin with the cause and then consider possible consequences, which in turn may serve as the causes of some future effects.

There are basically two main ways to organize a cause-and-effect essay: block and chain organization. In block organization, we first discuss all of the causes as a block and then we discuss all of the effects together as a block. In chain organization, we discuss a first cause and its effect and then a second cause and its effect, and a third cause and its effect, and so on, in a chain. The type of cause-and-effect organization will depend on our topic. A chain pattern is usually easier if the causes and effects are closely interrelated. If there is no direct cause-and-effect relationship, the block style may be easier. Some topics may require a combination of block and chain organizations.

The following passage analyzes the causes of Western culture's invasion into Chinese culture.

The Causes of the Culture Invasion

Both China and Britain are nations with rich culture. But the traditional Chinese festivals have existed on the land of China for a long history of thousands of years, while English festivals have spread to China just for decades. However, at present, some English festivals such as Christmas and Valentine's day seems to be more popular in China. How can they invade our traditional festivals and even substitute Chinese traditional festivals in such a short period of time? Take all the factors into account, the culture invasion is not a coincidence but necessity. There are a number of causes that contribute to this phenomenon.

The Changes of People's Notions and Taste

With the development of the economy, the world is growing toward the direction of a global country. The modern communication technology and the convenient transportation have broken the barriers of the international communication. A big change is taking place in Chinese society with more and more people watching overseas blockbusters, eating Western style foods and worshiping the famous stars from the Hollywood. The economic globalization has promoted the cultural globalization greatly. Chinese people tend to accept foreign culture including their food, their language, their styles, and festivals as well. When the foreign festivals are in their full swing in China, the weather-beaten traditional Chinese festivals fade out silently without being noticed. The youth claim that foreign festivals are more open and the celebrating activities are more flexible that they can be celebrated in many exciting and simple ways, such as sending red roses, chocolates, greeting cards to each other, decorating Christmas trees, holding parties, etc. However, having Chinese traditional festivals is complex and troublesome, and some even regard the reunion of festivals as a heavy burden that will waste a lot of time.

The Impact of the Influential Commercial Activities to the Cultural Invasion

Foreign festivals are becoming popular in China, because merchants rack their brains to make use of these chances to make big profits. When a foreign festival is coming, merchants find every means to promote sales of their products. They advertise their products on television, newspapers, magazines, and Internet; they hold all kinds of activities to attract consumer with loud music, alluring candle lit meals, charming balls, loving chocolates and romantic roses.

The Effect of Education and Media

The invasion of the foreign festivals is typically presented by the younger generations, especially students. In terms of education, the popularity of English teaching has brought the knowledge of foreign festivals to many people, especially the students. Secondly, the lack of traditional culture has led the younger generations negatively. They only know Christmas and the Valentine's Day but they have not much knowledge about traditional Chinese festivals such as "Qixi", also called Chinese lover's day, and "Chongyang", etc. They are familiar with the Christmas trees, the festival parties, chocolates and roses, but they have no idea about the connotations of the spring festivals, the mid-autumn day, etc. As regard to the mass media, they publish large pages of news and information about the foreign festivals but mention less words about the traditional Chinese ones.

Due to the changes of people's notions, commercial activities, and the influence of education and mass-media, foreign festivals are becoming more and more popular, while traditional Chinese festivals are paid less attention.

2. Comparison-and-contrast

Technically speaking, comparisons reveal similarities and differences between items, and contrasts are concerned only with differences. In practice, however, comparisons suggest likeness, and contrasts point out differences.

Comparison-and-contrast is a very common and useful pattern in developing an essay. We use it to explain or evaluate something. We can explain the similarities and differences between foreign festivals and Chinese ones. However, very often we use this pattern for the purpose of evaluation: to show that one book or movie is superior to another, or that a job offer is better than another. To make our purpose distinctive, after a comparison and contrast, we should not forget to make a judgment in the conclusion.

In comparison and contrast, there is one important rule for us to follow: only things of like nature and items in the same general class can be compared or contrasted.

There are two basic ways to organize a comparison and contrast essay: point-by-point organization or the block organization. In the former, we discuss one point of the features of the two items or subjects and then move to another; in the latter, we discuss all the features of one item and then the features of another. The following passage compares two novels *Pride and Prejudice* and *Little Women*.

Jane Austen, one of the most prominent writer in the 19th century finished her famous works *First Impression* and then changed its name into *Pride and Prejudice* in 1812. This novel talks about several love stories, exposing the money worship nature of capitalist marriage system deeply.

About half a century later, *Little Women*, written by Louisa May Alcott, came into being, whose target is on the daily life of the Marches. After reading the whole book, readers may be deeply impressed by the excellent personalities of the four sisters: pursuing self-independence, advocating self-discipline and loving the family.

The two books both deal with the love stories of several ladies. So it's as if that there are something similar between the two books. However, as a matter of fact, the relationship between love and kinship and property and marriage reflected in the books are totally different. *Pride and Prejudice* is endowed with comic atmosphere—"brisk, bright and splendid"(Zhuhong, 1997). But *Little Women* is overflowing with miss for the family caused by departure, the bitterness of hard working caused by poor life, and the depression caused by dreams that can't be realized at one time. The different atmosphere shown in the books is closely related to the different structure of personalities in the novels, which, however, have a close connection with family education.

At first different family education between the two families gives rise to different personalities of children. Let us have a look at the two novels. Mr. Bennet is a country gentleman, but he married a silly and ignorant woman. To avoid his wife's chattering, he often shut himself in his study, neglecting educating his children. Among the five daughters, except Jane and Elizabeth the other three girls are like their mother. Therefore, they are silly and dizzy as their mother, flirting with men as one of their big interest. As a mother, Mrs. Bennet is irresponsible, for her ultimate goal is to marry off the five daughters, and the ultimate interest is to call on friends. She never endeavors to educate her children with ethics and nurture them into well-being and graceful ladies. Money dominates her mood and action. She is even blind to her daughter's inappropriate behavior and proud of youngster's cohabitation. As a parent, she is responsible for the three younger daughter's superficial characters.

As the eldest daughter, Jane is attractive and innocent but sensitive to nothing. In her eyes, all people are nice, which for most people's part, may be her advantage. But the author maintains that it's a flaw in her character for she can't tell other's shortcomings, which proves her limitation in her judgement and ethical levels.

As the heroine of the novel, Elizabeth displays her charming personality in many aspects. She is deeply influenced by her father, inheriting his humor and sarcastic skills. But all her merits, in her stupid mother's eyes, turn into drawbacks. We can't deny that she is also branded with capitalism. At first, she is attracted by charming Wickham. After experiencing many incidents, some changes happen in her minds. Examine from inner world, she began to face reality both on her herself and others, showing her embarrassment, braveness and flexibleness. This transition has turned into a kind of virtue surpassing ranks.

However, in Little Women, the Marches set good examples for their children, which has favorable influence on their children both in their growth and personality. Being gentle and smart, Mr. March makes all his efforts to achieve self-improvement. In his spare time, he also shut himself in the study as Mr. Bennet does, indulging himself in his utopia fantasy. But he is still the backbone of the family. And his wife, unlike Mrs. Bennet, is a good woman with refinement who knows how to educate children. They never criticize when their daughters felt depressed because of doing something wrong or coming across some difficulty, but inculcate them by their own experience. With regard to heroes in the novel, they learn from each other, discovering merits on others and find their own flaws and correct them. No matter Meg, who relishes luxurious life of Joe who tends to have her full wing and be ill-tempered, or Beth who is timid and shy or Amy who is vain, they all use such a way to recognize and explore their flaws on personality. Therefore, their love for each other become deeper and deeper, which makes them cherish the kinship with each other.

The above passage compares the Bennet family and the March family. Because of their different family education, the characters of their children are different, too.

3. Division-and-Classification

To divide is to break a thing down into its parts; to classify is to show how these parts relate to the whole. In an essay developed by division-and-classification, we are doing the work of logically dividing a broad subject into several categories or groups and discussing them one after another.

Division and classification work well together in developing an essay that classifies and explains. In such an essay, the introduction normally states the thesis and lets the readers know the categories or classes into which the subject is divided or classified. The body paragraphs present each category or subclass in order, and the conclusion reinforces the thesis statement. Look at the following example.

The Classification of Loanwords

Loanwords are a common phenomenon in every language in the world. Loanwords, also called borrowing words, mean absorbing words or phrases from other languages. Loanwords from Chinese are a product of cultural contact between Chinese and English.

Loanwords can be classified into many types as the following.

(1) Politics.

Relate to some Chinese government, official terms, a series of political activities, dynasties, emperors and many other terms, such as the Taiping Upspring(太平天国起义)— *the peasants' revolt in 1851—1864, dazibao*(大字报)*, yamen*(衙门)*, etc.*

(2) Economics.

Some words indicate metrology, a unit of currency and terms of occupations, such as yuan(元)*, renminbi*(人民币)*, citizen-managed teacher*(民办教师)*, etc.*

(3) History and culture.

For instance, Confucianism(儒学)*,the four books and the five classics*(四书五经)*, feng shui*(风水)*,kowtow, ching ming*(清明)*, putonghua*(普通话)*, and so on.*

(4) *Region ethnic groups*.

Relate to geographical locations, historic sites, and minorities. For instance, Pekingese (北京人), *szechuanese*(四川人), *the Great Wall, the Summer Palace, and so on.*

(5) *Daily life*.

In foods, there are jiaozi(饺子), *chow mein*(炒面), *wonton*(馄饨), *wuliangye*(五粮液), *moutai*(茅台), *litchi*(荔枝), *bird's nest*(燕窝), *chopsuey*(杂碎), *and so forth.*

In clothes, there are Sun Yet-san(孙中山), *cheongsam*(旗袍), *tea gown*(宽松女袍), *Chinese jacket*(唐装), *and so forth.*

(6) *Arts and religions*.

It mainly focuses on some musical instruments, dramas, and dances. For example, pipa (琵琶), *Beijing opera*(京剧), *yangko*(秧歌), *pinyin*(拼音), *and the like.*

In religion, there are Panchen lama(班禅喇嘛), *wuwei*(无为), *yinyang*(阴阳), *and the like.*

(7) *Some words in special times*.

Such as paper tiger(纸老虎), *great leap forward*(大跃进), *cultural revolution*(文化大革命), *gang of four*(四人帮), *running dog*(走狗), *one country two systems*(一国两制), *four modernizations*(四个现代化), *iron rice bowl*(铁饭碗), *and the like.*

4. Exemplification

Many statements need to be illustrated and clarified by examples. Otherwise, they only give a hazy notion to the audience. They all need to be explained or proved. If most of the general statements of an essay are illustrated or clarified by examples, we say that this essay is developed by exemplification or illustration.

Good examples help to clarify writers' thought by making the general specific, and the abstract concrete. They also add interest and help to persuade or convince the reader. We attach great importance to the arrangement of our examples to make them serve well. If the examples occur chronologically, the obvious arrangement is in the order in which they happened. Another method of organization is importance order. Normally the less important examples are put first and then the most important ones are put at the end.

The organization of an essay developed by exemplification is relatively straightforward. The introduction brings forth the thesis statement, and the body of the essay presents a series of examples to support it. The conclusion reinforces the thesis statement. Look at the following example about different features of good slogans.

Rhetorical features

Rhetorical features contain many aspects. To be precise, such as metaphor, personification, etc. All of these can add spices to an essay — making it more fascinating and attractive. Similarly, when such devices are used in advertisement, they will exert magic power, as its variation of patterns and emotion kills two birds with one stone. Because selective part use of them gives readers a sense of novelty and a deep impression.

Alliteration

Alliteration means "the use of the same letter or sound at the beginning of words that are close together" (Oxford Advanced Learner's English-Chinese Dictionary). Like in a song or a poem, the harmony of rhymes has a magic power to recall the part easily and rises up to audible image. It is often used in commercials to make their slogans easier to comprehend and recall, because of its beauty of rhyme scheme and poetic pattern. For example.

(1) Beautiful beyond belief. —American Motors Corp

(2) Pick up the pack, picked at the peak of perfection. —Polar, frosted foods

The first example represents us an attractive and durable car, and the initiated letter "b" models the sound of a speedy car zooming past the audience. How beautiful and fast it is! And five words in the second example are all initiated with "p", it simulates the sound cracking a crispy object. So the target audience will be allured by such a pack of such brand of food which is crispy and pleasant to the palate.

Repetition

Repetition is always used to emphasize, so as to express a strong emotion to move the prospective consumers, to let them share the same feeling. The repeated part can be only a letter, a word, or even a phrase or a whole sentence. It seems dull for lacking new contents, but on the contrary, it draws the readers' attention to the repeated part where the most important points lies. For example.

(3) Keep you income coming in. —American National Bank

(4) Saves shaving seconds and second shavings. —Perma-Sharp Manufacturing

From the third example, we may be allured by the slogan to deposit our savings in the American Ntional Bank. We can not only be assured of its safety, but also get interest from the bank. And at the first sight of the fourth example, maybe readers will be confused, however, after looking over and thinking twice, we can't help admiring the slogan-makers, as it gives readers a laconic but detailed description of such goods—good quality and economy.

Climax

Climax is a special form of parallelism. If we say repetition is a progress, climax is a sudden point. It is the highest point of the part. Sometimes it just emphasizes the last part: it makes the whole episode important to show one subject sometimes. For example:

(5) Think once. Think twice. Think bike.

(6) Wash easier, dry faster, absorb more, wear longer.

The fifth example puts weight on the last phrase "Think bike". Think twice means consider carefully, but "Think bike" follows it, so evidently the emotion of it is much stronger and acute. So this public interests advertisement slogan warns the drivers of the safety of the riders. And the sixth example shows us four strong points of this brand of diaper.

Lexical and spelling deviation

In professional language aspects, these deviations don't conform to the rules of the language. Without the contents, it makes no sense. But when to be pursuit of attention value and directive function, they are welcome. Because they can offer people a sense of novelty and fresh, as well as a sort of fun. We can just admire the magic power of words, we can read the meaning between the lines. For example:

(7) Go well, go Shell.

(8) *The coffee-er coffee.*

(9) *RELy on REL for real RELief.*

These three are the combination of rhetorical features, such as rhymes, repetition and alliteration, lexical and spelling deviation. Shell is a brand name of tire, so we can see from the seventh example the good quality — tough of it. In the eighth example, the first coffee is regarded as an adjective. The proper usage of comparative degree of coffee implies the indescribable good flavor of this kind of coffee. REL is a sort of medicine. So the ninth example successfully emphasizes that REL is reliable.

5. Definition

In real life we have to define some terms we are using to avoid misunderstanding in communication. When the term is abstract, ambiguous, or controversial, we will try to explain it with more words. If the explanation turns out to be more than one paragraph in writing, we are developing an essay by definition, or exactly, by an extended definition. In a paper developed by definition, we are answering questions "What is it" or "What does it mean". To answer these two questions, we may employ examples, divide the topic into different classes, compare and contrast the term with synonyms, and talk about the causes and effects, or the process of an interesting story caused by this term. That is always the case, in which we start our writing by defining something, and then extend to some other ways to help. The following is a model essay developed by an extended definition.

Pragmatic Failure

Jenny Thomas notes that pragmatic failure has occurred on any occasion "on which the hearer perceives the forces of the speaker's utterances as other than the speakers intended she or he should perceive it." (Jenny Thomas, 1983) For example:

A: Do you know who caught the fire last night?

B: No, it's not me.

A: Oh, I don't mean that.

Actually, A only wanted to know who had caught fire, but B perceived the forces of A's utterance as stronger than A had intended. So B responded very severely. In his case pragmatic failure often happens.

According to Thomas, there are two types of pragmatic failure: pragmalinguistic failure and sociopragmatic failure, which I will talk about in detail next.

Pragmalinguistic Failure

Each culture has a set of norms regarding the appropriateness of different types of expressions and conversational strategies. In cross-cultural communication, pragmatic failure occurs when the non-native speakers are not capable of using the target language satisfactorily to convey their intentions. It is often the case that language learners tend to transfer from their native tongue into the target language expressions which are semantically or syntactically equivalent, but which have different communicative conventions. When they converse with the native speakers, they usually fail to make their meanings understood because their utterances, in one way or another, violate the principles or deviate from the conventions of the target language. The pragmatic force they map onto a given linguistic token or structure is systematically different from that most frequently assigned to it by native speakers. As a result, the hearer may either accept an illocutionary force which is not the intended one or find the utterance meaningless or inappropriate, for it does not fit the contexts. Pragmatic failure thus committed by Thomas is named pragmalinguistic failure. Below is a good example of this kind of failure.

(A Chinese college student works as a secretary in the International Computer Engineering Corporation. One day she worked very late. Her boss felt satisfied with her excellent work and thanked her.)

Boss: Thanks a lot. That's a great help.

Secretary: Never mind.

What the secretary wanted to express is something like "Don't mention it" or "You're welcome", but she used "Never mind" instead. In English, "Never mind" is often used to acknowledge an apology and is used by the person addressed to minimize the seriousness of the offense. The illocutionary force of "never mind" is consolatory. Apparently, the secretary misconveyed her intention by the use of the inappropriate expression in the particular situation. Thus, the deviation of "never mind" form the English pragmatic rules may account for the pragmalinguistic failure.

Pragmalinguistic failure is more a linguistic problem than a pragmatic one since it has little to do with the non-native speaker's perceptions of what constitutes appropriate linguistic behavior and a great deal to do with knowing how to apply the highly conventionalized usage of the target language.

Sociopragmatic Failure

The term sociopragmatic failure, again by Thomas, is used to refer to the cases which the non-native speakers do not have good knowledge of the sociocultural background of the target language. Some of their judgments "concerning the size of imposition, cost, benefit, social distance and relative rights and obligations"(Thomas, 1983) are different from those carried by the native speakers. Therefore, their linguistic behavior is socially inappropriate in the target language using community. For example:

(A Chinese woman scholar, who was visiting the United States, was complimented by the hostess at a party.)

Hostess: That's a lovely dress you have on.

Scholar: No, no. It's just a very ordinary dress.

The woman scholar's response is quite inappropriate in this situation because it would make the hearer embarrassed. Her reply conveys a message quite different from which is intended. It implies that the one paying the compliment does not know the difference between a lovely dress and an ordinary one. In other words, it means that the person does not have a good sense of taste or judgment; otherwise, how could she get so excited about an ordinary thing?

Obviously pragmatic failures like this example are more related to the cultural differences between English and Chinese. To English-speaking people, praise or compliment is to be accepted, generally with a remark like "thank you". However, when a Chinese is *praised or complimented, he/she would utter instant and repeated denials, or something like "you flatter me" or "I feel ashamed". It seems to him/her that acceptance of a compliment would imply conceit or lack of manners.*

Sociopragmatic failure, as opposed to pragmalinguistic failure, usually stems from cross-culturally different perceptions of what constitutes appropriate linguistic behavior and has to do with knowing what to say and whom to say it to. People coming from different sociocultural backgrounds tend to have very different value systems, which are manifested in speech as well as in other sorts of social behavior. These differences often lead to misunderstanding. What is even more critical is that the diversity in value system and in the ways in which they are expressed is usually not well understood. Therefore, sociopragmatic failure is almost inevitable if people coming from different backgrounds communicate to each other according to their own value systems.

Chapter 3　Writing the Paper

3.1　Writing the Abstract of a Thesis

3.1.1　What is an Abstract?

The abstract usually appears before the introduction of a paper, but it is often the last part of the paper to be written. For the convenience of reading and consultation, we write about it first since it is the first section presented in a paper.

The abstract is a summary of the study. For research purpose, an abstract makes readers quickly determine the content of a work and decide if the full text should be consulted. With published materials such as journal articles, abstracts are also important tools in an electronic search. Papers may be organized by subject matters based on the information of their abstracts.

A well-written abstract helps readers understand the purpose and value of the research work. It provides information concerning the following aspects: purpose of the study, the research questions to be addressed, the subjects involved, the instruments used to collect the data, the procedures for collecting and analyzing the data, and the actual findings or results. It should contain the most important words referring to method and content of the paper.

3.1.2　Structure of an Abstract

In fact, abstracts from almost all fields of study are written in more or less the same way. The types of information usually are included and their order are conventional, which usually appear in the following order.

1. Motivation or background information

Why do you care about the problem?

If the problem addressed in your thesis isn't obviously interesting or not widely recognized as important, it is better to put motivation first so as to arouse readers' attention. In this section, you should also point out the importance of your work, the difficulty of the area, and the impact it might have.

2. Question statement

What question are you trying to answer, and what is the scope of your thesis? The question statement is usually put forth after you tell the reader your motivation of the research. In some cases it may be appropriate to put the question statement before the motivation, but usually this only works if most readers already understand why the question is important.

3. Approach or method

How do you go about solving the problem? You may adopt such methods as simulation, prototype construction, analysis of field data, comparison. In this case you have to describe the approach including information like variables you control, ignore or measure, and the theoretical framework on which your research based.

4. Result

What's your answer to the question? Be concrete and specific with the result. Avoid vague terms in describing results such as very significant, small, etc.

5. Conclusions

Sometimes conclusions are discussed briefly in the abstract. What are the implications of your answer? Is it going to change our conventional concept, serve as a guideline for the problem?

3.1.3 Types of Abstract

Generally speaking, there are two kinds of abstract: descriptive and informative.

A descriptive abstract merely identifies area to be covered in the paper. It includes the purpose, methods, and scope of the research, but not the results, conclusions, or recommendations. It is usually very short that has only 100~200 words. Here is an abstract of a thesis about the development of China English.

To the general public, China English is a relatively new and serious concept, while in the fields of linguistics and translation a group of scholars have already made a study on it. Now most scholars hold that China English, based on the standard English, is a kind of variant of English to express things and concepts with Chinese characteristic. It is the product of the English language used in English-speaking countries combined with the unique Chineseness. Then, in the nation of China with a thousand-long history and civilization, how has China English come into being, grown and developed? This paper mainly focuses on the factors involved in the emergence and development of China English and it also explores people's attitude toward China English, and analyzes the trend and role of China English in China and the world.

An informative abstract summarizes the entire report and gives the reader an overview of the facts that will be laid out in detail in the paper itself. Usually it is longer than a descriptive abstract but rarely longer than one page. It communicates specific information from the paper, including the purpose, methods and scope of the paper, and provides the results, conclusions and recommendations.

In order to help students with their translation and assist teachers to find students' main problems with translation, this paper studies an English to Chinese translation exercise of the second year English majors in a university. The author studies in by collecting and sorting out the typical errors made by students and analyzing the causes of the errors guided by error analysis theory. The research adopts the basic translation criteria of TEM-8 in sorting out students' translation errors. According to the research, students' errors fall into these categories: confusion in denotative and connotative meanings of a word, unnatural Chinese expressions, problems in dealing with proper nouns, misinterpretation of sentence structures of the source text, etc. Then the thesis analyzes the underlying causes: students' lack of both translation theories and practice, and poor Chinese competence. It is hoped that more of this kind of research in both Chinese and English translation be done to guide translation teaching and practice.

In the above abstract, there are 158 words. It not only includes the purpose of the research (help students with their translation and assist teachers to find students' main problems with translation), the method adopted (students' error collection and analysis based on the concerning theory), the scope of research (an English to Chinese translation exercise of the second year English majors in a university), but also the findings (the categories of errors), conclusions (students' lack of translation theory and practice, and poor Chinese competence), and the recommendation (more of this kind of research in both Chinese and English translation should be done).

3.1.4 How to Write a Good Abstract

Abstracts are not easy to write. It puts high demand on the language use — being as brief and concise but informative as possible. On the other hand, it should also be self-contained — making sense alone without reference to the main text. So copying sentences directly from the sections of the paper does not work. Instead, students should select the most important information and synthesize it into clear, concise statements to give the reader an accurate preview of the contents of the paper. Here is the general way to organize the abstract.

1. Topic sentences

To be concise, an abstract may put the topic sentence right at the beginning which defines the goal and the scope of the research. The topic sentence is often written as the following examples.

(1) The purpose of this paper is ...

(2) The primary goal of this research is ...

(3) In this paper (article), we aim at ...

(4) The chief aim of the present work is to ...

(5) This paper discusses (studies, concerns, deals with) ...

(6) This paper argues (demonstrates) ...

(7) This paper explores (probes into, elaborates on, expounds) that ...

(8) This paper makes a comparison of (an overview of, an analysis of) ...

(9) In this paper, the author attempts to (intends to, proposes, contends, points out) that ...

2. Main body sentences

After defining the research goal and scope, the abstract has to provide further information about your research like the approach adopted, the procedures, the analysis or argumentation, etc.

It usually proceeds as the following examples.

(1) The method used in this is known as ...

(2) The technique we have used is referred to as ...

(3) The procedure can be described as ...

(4) The approach that has been adopted extensively is called ...

(5) Detailed information has been acquired by the authors using ...

(6) The research has recorded valuable data using the newly developed method. The underlying concept of this theory is ...

(7) The underlying principle of the theory is as follows ...

(8) The working theory which based on the idea is that ...

(9) The fundamental features of this theory are as follows ...

(10) The experiment, consisted of three steps, is described in ...

(11) We have carried out several experiments to test the validity of ...

(12) Recent experiments in this area have suggested that ...

(13) Special mention is given here to ...

3. Concluding sentences

In a sense, an abstract is a minitype of thesis. Its concluding sentences, serving as the conclusion of the thesis, have to indicate the results or findings of the research, explicate its application, significance and implication. It is usually written as the following examples.

(1) In conclusion, we state that ...

(2) In summing up it may be stated that ...

(3) Therefore, it can be concluded that ...

(4) The results of the experiment indicate that ...

(5) This fruitful work gives explanation of ...

(6) These findings of the research have led the author to a conclusion that ...

(7) Finally, the paper reflects on the current situation pertaining to ...

The abstract should be both in English and Chinese, each covering one page with the English one preceding the Chinese one. As the abstracts are not part of the text, they are neither numbered nor counted as a page.

3.1.5 The Extract of Key Words

Key words to the abstract are as the abstract to the thesis. They are the pith of the abstract. In one thesis there are usually two to six key words. Usually in the noun form, key words are generally the most frequently repeated words, part of the thesis statement or the focus of discussion. The first letter of each key words are not capitalized and a comma is used in between them. Here is an example.

This thesis attempts to look into the inner system of humorous utterances. Based on the principles of cognitive-pragmatics, this paper brings some examples of humorous utterances into the scope of relevance theory to explore the theoretical explanation for humorous utterance.

Key words: relevance theory, humorous utterance.

3.2 Writing the Introduction

As the first part or chapter in a thesis, an introduction is the first impression a thesis leaves to its readers. It is supposed to arouse the readers' interest, provide background information, introduce the topic under discussion or present the framework of the whole thesis, and so on. Although there is no rule as to how long an introduction should be, it should be written concisely and clearly because a lengthy one may either distract the thesis' focus or confuse the readers.

3.2.1 The Major Elements in an Introduction

The major elements in an introduction include three parts: ① introducing the topic to be discussed; ② focusing on an issue; ③ reviewing previous research. These three parts are discussed thoroughly in the following.

1. Introducing the topic

We can introduce the topic in a number of ways: we can start with an anecdote or ask a question to arouse readers' interest; we can provide some background information; we can quote an authority.

1) Providing background information

Usually, the introduction begins with statements of some background information. For example:

Animals are friends of human beings, and languages of all nations have a great number of words denoting animals. People associate their feelings and emotions, even happenings and natural phenomena with various animals. Many animals have become a kind of symbolism in people's mind, and this symbolism is reflected in language. For instance, sayings like "as busy as a bee" appear in many languages. However, these sayings do not necessarily coincide from one language to another due to different outlook of life and concept of beauty in different cultures.

The above example illustrates the importance of animals to human beings and different cultural connotations of animal words in different languages. These statements not only arouse the readers' interest but also provide important background information for the topic—the different cultural connotations of animal words in different languages.

2) Starting with an anecdote

You can start the introduction with an anecdote, a short story or some interesting facts to arouse the readers' interest and lead to your topic. For example.

During the period of the War to Resist US Aggression and Aid Korea, Premier Zhou had an interview with an American journalist who saw an American pen on the desk. So he asked maliciously, "Mr. Prime Minister, could you please tell me, why you Chinese having high aspiration and boldness of vision still use the pen made in USA?" Premier Zhou heard this and laughed, "Talking about this pen, there's a long history. This is not an ordinary pen. It's booty, in fighting against the US troops, sent by a Korean friend of mine, as a souvenir. I intended not to accept the pen, because I did not want to get a reward without deserving it. But beyond my expectation, the friend asked me to keep the pen as a memento of the event. I thought it significant, and accepted this pen which is manufactured in your country." Premier Zhou answered the question with the words "booty", "memento", "significant", which showed his wisdom. These pun words are so-called euphemism.

The above example begins the introduction with a suspenseful anecdote. It reveals the charm and significance of euphemism through a live example.

3) Quoting an authority

You can quote the ideas of some famous writers to support your research. In this way you can make your thesis more effective and convincing.

Researchers have shown that the words people speak may be far less important than the body language used when delivering verbal message. They estimate that less than 10 percent of the whole message understood by an audience is the actual content. Some 30 percent is attributed to the pitch and tenor of a person's voice and 60 percent to other forms of non-verbal communication from body language to facial expressions to hand gestures. (Charles Mitchell, 2000)

The above example shows the importance of non-verbal communication by quoting the words of Charles Mitchell.

2. Focusing on the issue

After introducing the topic, we need to focus on a specific research question, i.e., the purpose of the research. We can narrow down a general topic into a specific one. For example, if you are writing about a novel of Mark Twain, in the introductory section, you may provide some background information about the writer and his novels, and in this section, you will focus on a specific novel written by him. The following are two specific examples.

Example 1

The article tries to analyze the features of the subtitles of the movie Crouching Tiger Hidden Dragon in terms of time-space constraints, informative function and cultural factors, and then puts forward corresponding strategies for translation, with concrete examples for illustration.

Example 2

In this thesis, the author will discuss the differences of cultural connotations between Chinese and English animal words, and try to investigate the importance of the input of culture in vocabulary teaching.

3. Reviewing previous research

The English great scientist Newton once said, "If I have seen a little further, it is by standing on the shoulders of giants", which implies that any discoveries and inventions are not made by one individual alone but instead they are based on the researches conducted by predecessors. This is why related researches need to be reviewed in a thesis.

This section is usually called literature review. The purpose of literature review is to describe the history and present situation of the research area, and analyze the originality and inheritance of your research. It can be said that any research is the inheritance of the previous research.

In this section, you need to illustrate what are the differences between your research and previous research; how you formulate your own research design based on others' research; what are the theoretical background on which your research is based, etc. The fundamental purpose of this section is to convince readers that your research topic is worthy of research and your research design is appropriate.

Specially speaking, literature review includes the following parts: ① Defining the key terms; ② Providing theoretical background for your research; ③ Evaluating related research; ④ Formulating your own research design.

Literature review generally includes the above four aspects, but it should be noted that in actual writing, you may not obey this order and you may add more information or reduce these information according to your purpose, or personal preference.

Lastly, reviewing previous research doesn't necessarily belong to the introduction section. In many research papers, especially in complicated and long research papers, this section is often separated as an independent section titled as literature review.

1) Defining the key terms

Different researchers may give different definitions to the same term. Therefore, a key term usually has a lot of definitions given by different researchers according to different research perspectives and requirements. Before presenting your own definition, you need to list a few typical definitions given by famous researchers. However, only listing is not enough, you'd better evaluate briefly the different definitions and then present your own definition and explain how you form this definition, why you use this one instead of others. The following is an example.

What is language? Different researchers have different concepts. Webster's New World Dictionary offers several most frequently used scenes of the word "language", namely: ① human speech; ② the ability to communicate by this means; ③ a system of vocal sounds and combination of such sounds to which meaning is attributed, used for the expression or communication of thoughts and feelings; ④ the written representation of such a system. These definitions give the conceptual meanings of language and its representative forms.

The most typically and generally acceptable definition is: Language is a system of arbitrary vocal symbols used for human communication. This definition is mostly generalized and it distinguishes human language from any other animals' languages.

A famous Chinese linguist Zhao Shikai defined language from different angles: ① language is a social action and a carrier of information; ② language is a system of structure, it contains phonetics, vocabulary and meaning, morphology and syntax; ③ language is a social phenomenon because it is an instrument of human communication in a society; ④ language is a physiological phenomenon because it is connected with the organs of speech, the nervous system and muscular activities; ⑤ language is a psychological phenomenon because it is closely related to man's psychological activities; ⑥ language is also a physical phenomenon owing to the propagation of speech sounds. These definitions are comparatively complete and all-around. It defines language from different angles like linguistics, sociology, psychology, physics, etc.

On the basis of the above-mentioned points, language may be defined as follows: language is a system of symbols based on physiology, psychology and physics. It is a specific social action and a carrier of information used for human communication in a society.

In the above example, the author lists three kinds of definitions of language and then formulates his or her own definition. From his or her definition, it can be seen that he or she emphasizes the functions of language as an instrument for communication and a carrier of information.

2) Providing theoretical background

Research question usually derives from a certain theory, or is related with the theory. So it is necessary to explain some theory which is closely related with your research question. For example, when you are writing a paper about the cultural differences between Chinese and English color words, it is necessary to make clear the relationships between language and culture. Language belongs to culture and expresses cultural reality. It is the carrier and container of culture and as a mirror of culture, it is strongly influenced and shaped by culture. This theory provides the background information for the research paper because different color words have different cultural connotations, i. e. , language reflects culture. The following passage explains the relationships between language and culture in detail.

The relationship between language and culture is not just that between a part and a whole. It is much more complex than that. Language is the carrier and container of culture; language, as a mirror of culture, is strongly influenced and shaped by culture; language and culture is closely related, each influencing and shaping the other. As E. Sapir(1884), an American linguist, points out that a language can't exist in a "cultural vacuum", nor can it exist in a vacuum of practices and beliefs inherited from the society. As the carrier of culture, every language has its own system and structure. And every nation has its own living habits, thinking way, language psychology, behavior criterion, sense of worth, and cultural tradition.

3) Evaluating related research

This section is the most important part in literature review. It generalizes and sums up the previous research involved in the research area. What are the research findings so far achieved? What research questions or topics are still under research? It helps to make your research significant and convincing.

It's not inappropriate and impossible to list all the related research. An effective way is to choose those typical and important researches and record their research processes and research results.

After documenting the related research, you are required to evaluate them. You may discuss their contribution or deficiencies. Just because the research conducted so far is not enough or has deficiencies, your research seems to be significant and necessary.

There are mainly three ways of referring to other researchers' research. You can quote the original words of the researcher directly or indirectly; you can paraphrase other people's words; and you can summarize longer passages of texts.

(1) Direct or indirect quotations.

Quotations are not specific to literature review. An effective and persuasive research paper may quote a lot of ideas or thoughts given by famous writers or researchers. However, the background information on some subjects/topics may be too much and therefore you should choose the sources that best support your arguments.

When quoting some authoritative ideas, you should discuss the relationships between these ideas and your own investigation. A common problem is that many writers just fill their research papers with extensive quotations without discussing their relationships with the research, which can make the paper less coherent and logical and finally confuse the readers.

In quoting other people's ideas, you can use direct quotation, i.e., record other people's original words without any change, but you should use other people to indicate quotation. You can also use indirect quotation, i.e., express the ideas of other people in your own words. In indirect quotation, you don't have to use other people. Either in direct or indirect quotations, you should include the writers' names, the years in which the works are published and sometimes the pages.

The reporting verbs play an important role in conveying to readers your evaluation of the quotation. A verb like "say" or "write" is unmarked or neutral. It just states the fact that someone else has said or written something. But a verb like "criticize" or "object" is marked, i.e., it has an added meaning, in addition to only stating the fact. Read the following two examples.

Example 3

According to Hugh Rawson (1981), euphemism can be semantically divided into two types: the positive and the negative. The positive one can also be called stylistic one, which "inflate and magnify the word meaning, making the euphemized seem altogether grander and more important than they really are."

Example 4

Neaman (1983) pointed out that two psychological bases of euphemism were taboo and politeness. Politeness is a universal phenomenon in various languages ad cultures; it restrains people's action and speech, coordinates people's relationship. Therefore, it is one of the important factors people must pay attention to in order to achieve success in communication.

Example 1 can be called direct quotation, as it uses the author's original words, which are included in the parentheses. In example 2, the writer uses indirect quotation because he/she quotes other people's idea by using his or her own words. The quotation is introduced by the verb phrase "point out".

(2) Paraphrasing.

Paraphrasing is rewriting the original resources in your own words. You should not change the meanings contained in the original passage nor shorten it. For example, you can give synonyms for some of the words, change the passive structures into active ones or vice versa, change direct quotations into indirect ones, or write shorter or longer sentences than in the original materials.

(3) Summarizing.

A summary is a brief restatement of the essential thought of a longer composition. It reproduces the theme of the original with as few words as possible. When you write a summary, you should not interpret or comment. All you have to do is to give the gist of the author's exact and essential meaning. Usually, a summary is about one-third to one-fourth as long as the original passage. Therefore, you should omit the unimportant details and keep only those important ones. The summary should be written in your own words, and you should follow the logical order of the original passage.

After referring to the previous research, you should make some comments about them. You can point out any deficiencies in these researches. You can discuss any problems in previous research like research design, research samples or research results. Through discussing the deficiencies of previous research, you can prove the necessity and importance of your own research, and also connect your research with others'. Here is an example of literature review.

Euphemism has been used for a long time. It is also widely studied by Chinese and foreign scholars with great interest. In 1932, in a relatively long time in China, advocated by Chen Wangdao in his book An Introduction to Rhetoric (Xiucixue Fafan), euphemism was studied as a means of rhetorical devices. In 1983, Chen Yuan discussed euphemism in his book Socialinguistics in great details. From then on, more and more Chinese scholars who study foreign languages began to carry out some researches on this subject and published a large number of papers which made the study of euphemism step into a new stage. In recent years, Liu Chunbao has compiled A Dictionary of English Euphemisms, and it is regarded as an important work on euphemism. In English-speaking countries, American linguist Menken's The American Language and British linguist Hugh Rawson's A Dictionary of Euphemisms and Other Doubletalk are both extraordinary works on euphemism.

However, it is not difficult to find that most of these works deal with euphemism in a single language. They either treat euphemism as a rhetorical device or discuss the nature of euphemism. Few works or papers are devoted to the comparison of euphemism between two languages and get the corresponding translation strategies. In other words, most of the researches have been done in the linguistic field. As far as the author of this thesis is concerned, the discussion on the translation of euphemism is of great significance in cross-cultural communication. It will help the readers to overcome some barriers in understanding or translating euphemism.

The writer firstly reviews the study on euphemism by listing a few famous researchers and their works. Then he points out the deficiency of these researches: most of these works deal with euphemism in a single language and few works or papers are devoted to the comparison of euphemism between two languages and get the corresponding translation strategies. In this way, he justifies the need for his own research.

4) Formulating the Research Design

After reviewing other people's works and ideas, you can now present your own research design. You can put forward the general framework of your research including the purpose and the process. You may propose new or different ideas compared with others or just discuss the same topic from a new or different perspective, or your research design or methods are different from others. In a word, your research should be innovative in some way, because a valuable research paper should be innovative and creative. The following is an example.

This thesis attempts to offer some strategies for the translation of euphemism in English-Chinese and Chinese-English translation on the basis of Chen Hongwei and Li Yadan's translation criterion — "similarity in function and correspondence in meaning". Starting with the discussion on translation and culture, the thesis compares English and Chinese taboo words, and provides specific euphemisms that substitute taboo words with some translation strategies which may be helpful to the English learners and translators.

3.2.2 Summary

The introduction plays a vital role in the organization of information in a research paper. It fulfills a number of important functions including arousing readers' interest, focusing on a topic, reviewing previous works, discussing their deficiencies and finally formulating your own research design.

An introduction is normally kept short, since a lengthy one gives readers an impression of redundancy. You may include all the above-mentioned elements in the introduction, or you may add more or reduce some of these elements. You may not follow the order of the elements as presented in this book. However, you should keep a logical order in the introduction. The language in an introduction should be clear, specific and accurate. You also need to learn how to evaluate other people's works with these techniques like quoting, paraphrasing, and summarizing.

3.3 Conclusion

Conclusion is the final part of a research paper. Until now, readers have read the whole paper and have known the whole research process. However, readers may still feel it difficult to remember all the important points of the paper. Therefore, the main purpose of conclusion is to help readers review the main content of the paper completely. Some people may think that the body section has provided very detailed information, so the conclusion seems to be redundant and unnecessary. This view is certainly wrong because the conclusion sums up the whole paper by restating the main points covered in the paper, thus bringing the whole research into a natural end. Generally speaking, conclusion can give readers the deepest impression. Conclusion is also important for the thesis defense committee members to judge the quality of the paper. The judges will focus on the final part to make an initial judgment of the thesis.

Conclusion contains in summary from what has already been presented in the paper. Reference is made to different sections of the paper, and to the relationships between one part and another. Some conclusions may mention the deficiencies of the present research but most look into the future and discuss briefly the significance of their research in the field. On the whole, there are three elements in a conclusion: ① referring to the paper's sections in a summary statement; ② discussing some of the implications of the research in the wider context of investigation; ③ looking into the future for possible developments.

Example 5

Overseas investment and multinational operation of Chinese enterprises are brand-new practice. Their rising and development are the result of our country's practice of economic policy of reform and opening up to the outside world. After more than 20 years' development, Chinese enterprises' multinational operation has gained certain achievements. However, compared with Western developed countries, Chinese enterprises' multinational operation still has various problems in terms of its scale, international competition, and so on.

This thesis analyzes those problems and reasons of the problems from a microcosmic angle. Moreover, in view of these problems, the thesis concludes that we should study and learn from the experience of other country's multinational operation. Meanwhile, we should combine it with our country's whole developing strategy of national conditions and economic society, and put forward appropriate counter-measures to promote the development of Chinese enterprises' multinational operation. Seen from a microcosmic angle, Chinese enterprises should formulate feasible and realistic developing aims and implementing plans according to their own characteristics: to set down strategy for internationalization; to change the present mechanism of enterprises and establish modern operating system; to improve the innovation of technology and enhance the international competitive power of our enterprises; to improve the quality of human resource and train excellent international business personnel.

Example 6

To sum up, culture influences communication styles. Cultural styles can and do create misunderstandings in communication among people from different cultures. The major concern of this thesis has been to discuss the importance of pragmatic failure in intercultural communication. The thesis has argued that to be successful in international relationships, we must recognize differences as resources. An exact copy of us can only multiply our own flaws; the differences of others can provide a renewed resource of insight.

3.4 Revision

After you have written the first draft, you should make revisions about your research paper. Generally speaking, a good research paper should include three drafts: the first draft, the revised draft and the final draft.

In revising your research paper, you should first pay attention to the content, the organization, and the language of it, and then search for mistakes in spelling, grammar and punctuation. You should be concerned with the major matters of organization, the development of ideas, logic and continuity. Read through your paper carefully to see whether it flows smoothly. You may even want to read it out loudly, keeping in mind that if it does not sound good to you, it will not sound good to the reader. This may also be the time to determine if you need to add or delete information that will help strengthen the support for your thesis. Then, set aside your first draft for a day or two before revising. This will make it easier to view your work objectively and see any gaps or problems. The following questions give us a detailed checklist of the thesis.

1. Content   Look at the thesis as a whole

(1) Is the thesis statement focused sharply so that the reader know exactly what the controlling idea is?

(2) Does the introduction catch the reader's interest and lead to the thesis statement?

(3) Do the body paragraphs support our thesis? Do we have enough ideas, facts and information?

(4) Does the conclusion section summarize the whole thesis, reinforce the thesis statement, and leave a final comment or urge reader to do further research?

2. Organization   Look at the arrangement of the materials

(1) Does each paragraph deal with one point or aspect of the thesis statement and is that point expressed in a topic sentence?

(2) Are there any ideas that need to be expanded?

(3) Are there any ideas that are irrelevant and unrelated to the thesis statement?

(4) Are the paragraphs in the right logic order? Are there proper transitions between sentences, paragraphs or sections?

3. Language   Look at the words and sentences

(1) The words.

① Are there any words that are not appropriate for the topic or the style of the whole thesis?

② Are there any words or phrases which are directly translated from Chinese but which may mean something different in English?

③ Are there any collocations which may be incorrect because they are taken from Chinese?

(2) Sentences.

① Are there any redundancies, repetition in sentences?

② Are the sentences complete, concise, accurate, and appropriate?

③ Are there any structural and grammatical mistakes?

The content is the most important to a thesis, so you should check the content carefully. Firstly, you should check the thesis statement. The thesis statement is the backbone of the thesis. You may check it up by writing down the developed ideas of your thesis on a separate sheet of paper. If we simply can't sum up the main idea, we need to consider whether your thesis statement is specific enough to control the development of ideas or these ideas hold together to support your thesis to make the paper unified. Then you should check the introduction of your thesis. The introductory paragraph is like an advertisement that attracts or refuses the audience. An experienced writer may use some "hook" to catch the reader's interest and attract him to read through. You should check the body part of the thesis carefully to see if they contain enough support. We may jot down the main ideas in each paragraph to see whether we have employed enough material or information, convincing examples, facts and reasons to make your thesis clear to the reader. Lastly, you should check whether the conclusion part summarizes the main idea of the thesis, whether it highlights the significance of the research.

The organization of your thesis is also important, as we know that a thesis is an integrated whole consisting of closely connected small parts. We should check whether you have topic sentences and whether the main ideas are expressed clearly and completely. If you find any irrelevant or unrelated ideas, you should omit them to make the thesis concise. You should pay special attention to the logic order of your thesis. Don't make any logic mistakes. Finally, you should check whether you have used transitional words to make your thesis flow smoothly and naturally.

At last, you should check the language in your thesis. Because thesis writing is a kind of academic writing, the language should be formal, accurate, and concise. You should use technical and formal words but you may not want to make it too rigid or obscure. You should check whether there are any mistakes in spelling, grammar, diction, and punctuation.

In the following examples, let's compare the first draft and revised version of an introduction of a thesis.

The first draft

Introduction

Politeness, which is a social phenomenon, touches upon every aspect of life. It naturally comes into theorist's view in different perspectives. It is of great concern with sociologists, sociolinguists, social psychologist, etc. They probe into the content of politeness, its principle, its function, and its means. Here I mainly look into it from the <u>pragmatics'</u> angle. Generally speaking, politeness can be considerate of others in order to achieve some social goals, such as maximizing the benefit to oneself and others, minimizing the face-threatening nature of a social act, etc. The ultimate goal of politeness is "the attainment of comity"(Leech, 1983). It is true that people can achieve this kind of social purpose by many means, but non-verbal and verbal expressions may be regarded as <u>mainly</u> two tools in presenting the degree of politeness. Between them, verbal expression takes priority over the others, which is to be a focus in this paper.

Business negotiation is a complex human activity, which plays an important role in economic interactions. As a rule, the negotiating parties have to make a decision about their respectively independent objectives. Herb Cohen, an American famous negotiating master, points out that a successful negotiation does not mean "winning by defeating the other party, but winning by getting what both parties want". For the economic interest, both parties have to mutually compete against each other, but simultaneously have to cooperate with each other. If both parties go to extremes, the negotiation is doomed to break down.

It is indeed worthwhile to study how negotiators get along with each other. In order to avoid the deadlock or failure of negotiation, the meditation of interpersonal relationship is one of the most important factors. In the course of business negotiation, the harmonious, friendly and cooperative atmosphere can better the negotiating conditions that keep the negotiation going on smoothly. Thus it is rewarding for the negotiators to create a friendly and cooperative situation through some appropriate strategies and tactics. Among them, politeness can work as one of those effective negotiation strategies, which is "the broad plan or technology used to obtain the outcomes desired from the negotiation and the resultant agreement"(Wall, 1985).

Basic to the universality of politeness in language usage is a rational model person, who is able to choose an appropriate way in which he can maintain the mutual faces in the most efficient way possible. He must manage to avoid face-threatening act in accordance with the politeness principle as against the cooperative principle. If he acts in some cases as the cooperative principles supposes, he is easy to threaten the others' face. So the politeness principle would be suitable, for the politeness principle manages to maximize benefits to others and to minimize benefits to self. In the course of business negotiation, conflict occurs easily. A negotiator endeavors to be the model person. On the one hand, he tries to cater to the other's opinion, attitude and face wants; on the other hand, he manages to maintain his own face at the same time. Under this circumstance, the rational model negotiator must take some appropriate strategies and language. Among them, such politeness language strategies as vagueness, euphemistic presentation, understatement, and compliments are some effective politeness ones, which are to be explicated in my dissertation.

Through the explication of the politeness theory and its language strategies, we attempt to improve human communicative competence, human trust, and research into the intrinsic quality of business negotiations, and increase the successful chances of business negotiations. As a result, the strategy of politeness language can to some extent guide business negotiations.

The revised version

Introduction

Politeness, which is a social phenomenon, touches upon every aspect of life. It naturally comes into theorist's view in different perspectives. It is of great concern with sociologists, sociolinguists, social psychologist, etc. They probe into the content of politeness, its principle, its function, and its means. Here I mainly look into it from the pragmatic angle. Generally speaking, politeness can be considerate of others in order to achieve some social goals, such as maximizing the benefit to one self and other, minimizing the face-threatening nature of a social act, etc. The ultimate goal of politeness is "the attainment of comity" (Leech, 1983). It is true that people can achieve this kind of social purpose by many means, but nonverbal and verbal expressions may be regarded as mainly two tools in presenting the degree of politeness. Between them, verbal expression takes priority over the others, which is to be a focus in this paper.

Business negotiation is a complex human activity, which plays an important role in economic interactions. As a rule, the negotiating parties have to make a decision about their respectively independent objectives. Cohen Herbert, an American famous negotiating master, points out that a successful negotiation does not mean "winning by defeating the other party, but winning by getting what both parties want". For the economic interest, both parties have to mutually compete against each other, but simultaneously have to cooperate with each other.

In the course of business negotiation, conflict occurs easily. A negotiator endeavors to be the model person. On the one hand, he tries to cater to the other's opinion, attitude and other face wants; on the other hand, he manages to maintain his own face at the same time. Under this circumstance, the rational model negotiator must take some appropriate strategies and language. Among them, such politeness language strategies as vagueness, euphemistic presentation, understatement, and compliments are some effective politeness ones, which are to be explicated in my dissertation.

Through the explication of the politeness theory and its language strategies, we attempt to improve human communicative competence, human trust, and research into the intrinsic quality of business negotiations, and increase the chances of successful business negotiations. As a result, the strategy of politeness language can to some extent guide business negotiations.

As an introduction, the first draft is too long and redundant. The first paragraph gives a definition of the pragmatic principle of politeness; the second paragraph illustrates business negotiation; the third paragraph emphasizes the importance of using the strategy of politeness in business negotiations; and the fourth and fifth paragraphs mainly discusses how a business negotiator uses politeness principle in business negotiations and the purpose and functions of politeness principle.

The logic sequence is very clear: it starts from politeness and business negotiations and the importance of politeness principle, and then how to use politeness in business negotiations. However, the fourth paragraph is too long and redundant because it discusses in detail how a negotiator uses politeness principle in business negotiations. This should be the purpose or goal of the research, but now it seems that it is the result of the research. If the result is clear, what is the use of the research? Therefore, the fourth paragraph is redundant and unnecessary. Besides, there are a number of grammatical mistakes in the introduction, which are underlined. By comparison, the revised introduction is clear and concise. It follows the logic sequence of the introduction.

In the following examples, let's compare the first draft and revised version of the conclusion of a thesis.

The first draft

Conclusion

To be successful in international relationships, we must recognize difference as resource. An exact copy of us can only multiply our own flaws—the differences of others can provide a renewed resource of insight. If we hope to shift between cultures with swiftness and ease, we've got to master the pragmatic principles, have a good grasp of different social culture, and develop our pragmatic and culture difference awareness and combine language study so as to understand each other well and cooperate with each other better and make successful communication.

The revised version

Conclusion

To sum up, cultures influence communication styles. Cultural styles can and do create misunderstanding in communication among people from different cultures. The major concern of this thesis has been to discuss the importance of pragmatic failure in intercultural communication. The thesis has argued that to be successful in international relationships, we *must regard difference as resource. An exact copy of us can only multiply our own flaws; the differences of others can provide a renewed resource of insight. If we hope to shift between cultures with swiftness and ease, we have to master the pragmatic principles, have a good grasp of different social culture, and develop our pragmatic and cultural awareness and combine language study so as to understand each other better and cooperate with each other better and make successful communication.*

With the more and more cross-cultural communication in the world, it is more urgent to study intercultural pragmatics with more care and respect for different cultures. As this thesis only studied a small part of pragmatic failure in intercultural communication, there are many deficiencies and it is not all-around. In order to completely explore the relationship between language and culture and achieve successful communication, I hope that more people would like to take part in this activity and more investment would be put to this project.

3.5 Documentation

Documentation of direct and indirect quotations in no way diminishes the originality of your work. Rather, documentation allows your reader to see the materials you used to reach your conclusions, to check your interpretations of sources, to place your work in a tradition of inquiry, and to locate further information on your topic. Your contribution consists of imposing your own order on the sources you use and drawing an original conclusion from them.

Plagiarism, a word derived from the Latin for kidnapping that now means the use of another person's ideas or wording without giving appropriate credit, results from inaccurate or incomplete attribution of material to its source. Ideas, as well as the expression of those ideas, are considered to belong to the person who first puts them forward. Therefore, when you incorporate in your paper either ideas or phrasing from another writer, whenever you quote directly or indirectly, you need to indicate your source accurately and completely. Either intentional or unintentional, plagiarism can have serious consequences — not only academic, in the form of failure or expulsion but also legal, in the form of lawsuits. Plagiarism is taken seriously because it violates the ethics of the academic community.

You must document any fact or opinion that you read in one of your sources, whether you first discovered the idea there or you have assimilated it so thoroughly that it seems to be your own. Some exceptions to this rule are facts that are common knowledge (e.g. Beijing is the capital of China) and facts that can be verified easily.

3.5.1 Format of Citation and Notes

There are three basic styles of documentation. The first one is Chicago Manual widely used in humanities and social science. The second one is APA (The American Psychological Association) style mainly used in psychology and linguistics. The third one is MLA (Modern Language Association) widely used in humanities. In choosing the style of documentation, we follow the conventions of our field of study and of the journals in which we are going to publish our papers.

MLA style is used for identifying research sources, which concerns itself with the mechanics of writing, such as punctuation, quotation, and documentation of sources. MLA style has been largely adopted by schools, academic departments, and instructors for nearly half a century. Its guidelines are currently used for over 125 scholarly and literary journals, newsletters, and magazines; by hundreds of smaller periodicals; and by many universities and commercial presses. MLA style is commonly followed not only in the United States but in Canada and other countries as well, the Chinese translation was published in 1990.

Notes may be placed at the bottom of the page on which the references (footnotes) occur or given in a consecutive series at the end of the paper (endnotes) or be in parenthesis at the end of the sentence (in-text notes or parenthetical quotations). There are three styles for notes: MLA style, APA style and CM Documentary style.

MLA style follows the parenthetical-reference system in documentation that consists of two items, the reference citations in text, and a works-cited list. The reference citations should include the last name of the author and the page number, without an intervening comma. As a style for humanities, MLA cares much for the readability of the paper and so contains only enough information to enable readers to find the source in the works-cited list.

On the other hand, **APA**, as a style for social sciences, cares more for timeliness of research and so contains the period of time of the source. It follows a principle that documentation should be entered in a way that makes the identity of the source entirely clear while avoiding duplication and unnecessary clutter. APA style requires two elements for citing sources: reference citations in text, and a reference list. The parenthetical references include the author's last name and the year of publication enclosed in parentheses. The parenthesized author name and year of publication are punctuated by a comma. Citations are placed within sentences and paragraphs so that it is clear what information is being quoted or paraphrased and whose information is being cited. When citing a specific part of a source, page numbers for quotations are always given. Note that the words page and chapter are abbreviated to "p." and "chap." in text citations.

You can see the difference between APA and MLA parenthetical citations from the following examples.

Example of MLA　　Darwin used the metaphor of the tree of life "to express the other form of interconnectedness—genealogical rather than ecological" (Gould 14).

Example of APA　　In teaching, the instructors should not only delve into teaching itself, but also try all means to strengthen the learners' motivation (Gui, 1985, p. 229).

Traditionally, the **CM Documentary** style is regarded as a note system, for unlike MLA and APA styles, it places bibliographic citations at the bottom of a page (footnotes) or at the end of a paper (endnotes). CM style follows the note-bibliography system in documentation that consists of three items: the first reference, subsequent reference, and bibliography. Here are the guidelines.

A first note reference to a book should include the author, the title, the place, the publisher, the date of publication, and the page number.

(1) Author. The author's name should be in its usual order and not inverted as in a bibliography entry. The author's name is followed by a comma.

(2) Title. The title of a book should be underlined or italicized. The title of a short story or an article should be put in quotation marks. The title is not followed by a comma or a period but the first half of the parentheses.

(3) Place of publication. The place of publication, either a city or a town, should be put in the parentheses, and the place is followed by a colon. If the state or province where the city or town located is also mentioned, we should put the city or town before the state or province and put a comma in between and a colon after the state or province.

(4) Publisher. The press, company or publishing house is also put in the parentheses and is followed by a comma. Note that UP is used for "university press" and P for "press".

(5) Date of publication. The date is put after the publisher and is followed by the other half of the parentheses.

(6) Page number. The page number is put outside the parentheses and is followed by a period.

So items (3), (4) and (5) in a note are put in the parentheses. Before and after the parentheses there should be no punctuation.

The following are some samples of first notes for the sources cited. We should notice the differences in the use of punctuation between a bibliography entry and a note entry.

Any further, or subsequent, references to this work in the footnotes are presented as shortened citations. A shortened citation consists of the family name, and the title of the work (shortened if more than four words).

The bibliography provides approximately the same citation details with the Chicago notes. However, there are several significant differences between them.

All works in the bibliography should be alphabetized according to the author's last name; if it is not given, simply go on to the next item in order and use that to alphabetize the entry.

(1) For each entry the author's surname or family name comes before the given name, with a comma in between.

(2) The location of publication, publisher, and year of publication are not put in parentheses.

(3) Periods are used to separate items.

(4) For each entry the first line is not indented, subsequent lines are indented 5 spaces.

The following are the examples.

(1) First reference.

Johanna Wyn and Rob White, " The Concept of Youth," in *Rethinking Youth* (Sydney: Allen and Unwin, 1997),11.

(2) Subsequent reference.

Wyn and White, " The Concept of Youth," 11.

(3) Bibliography.

Johanna Wyn and Rob White. " The Concept of Youth. " in *Rethinking Youth*. Sydney: Allen and Unwin, 1997.

As mentioned, footnotes appear at the bottom of each page of the text of our paper and endnotes are placed in one long list on a separate page or pages immediately after the text, and in-text notes should be placed as near to the material as is possible without disrupting the flow of the sentence.

If we choose to have footnotes, we should make sure that we keep numeral sequence throughout the paper and should not begin with a new footnote number 1 on each page. We should separate the footnotes from our text, leaving two lines of space.

The first line of every note is indented from the left-hand margin (usually the same number of spaces as paragraph indentations in the body of our paper), but any subsequent lines of the same note are brought to the left-hand margin. The numeral for a footnote or an endnote should be placed before the note, half a space higher than the note entry. There should be one space between the numeral and the note entry.

You are advised to consult your instructor and university regulations for the noting method you should use. The following are the typical parenthetical citations in MLA style.

1) Place and punctuation of citations

(1) A parenthetical citation should be placed as near to the material as is possible.

Even though the overall translation activity is a kind of communicative behavior between the source text and the target text via the translator (Jang, 14), the coding-decoding mechanism, cannot fully explain how contents are transformed, distorted, lost or suppressed in the process of communication (Sperber and Wilson, 145-151).

(2) When material from one source and the same page numbers is used throughout a paragraph, use one citation at the end of the paragraph rather than a citation at the end of each sentence.

(3) Parenthetical citations usually appear after the closing quotation mark of the sentence, and place the parenthetical citation after the final punctuation mark in set-off quotation. One space separates the period from the reference, which is not followed by a period.

According to Schele and Freidel, the Maya represented each point of the compass with a different color.

East was red and the most important direction since it was where the sun was born. North, sometimes called the "side of heaven", was white and the direction from which the cooling rains of winter came... West, the leaving or dying place of the sun, was black. South was yellow (66).

(4) For an ellipsis at the end of a sentence, the parenthetical reference follows three points indicating the omission and precedes the period.

Schele and Freidel explain that for the Mayas " the Underworld was sometimes called Xibalba..." (66).

2) Basic rules for different sources

The MLA system of parenthetical citations depends heavily on authors' names and page numbers. Because some of today's electronic sources have unclear authorship and lack page numbers, they present a special challenge. Nevertheless, the basic rules are the same for both print and electronic sources. Most parenthetical citations include the last name of the author and the page number, without an intervening comma.

(1) Author's name in text.

When the author's name appears in the introduction to the material, we need not repeat the name within parentheses.

Corder, a well-known linguist, held that using a language is a psychological process and so is the learning of a foreign language (320).

(2) Two or three authors.

Name the authors in the signal phrase, or include their last names in the parenthetical reference. When three authors are named in the parentheses, separate the names with commas.

CDA is, therefore, analysis with attitude. It proclaims an interest and sets an agenda, as Fairclough and Wodak make clear: "What is distinctive about CDA is both that it intervenes on the side of the dominated and oppressed group and against dominating groups and that is openly declares the emancipatory interests that motivate it." (259)

(Fairclough and Wodak 259)

(Fairclough, Wodak , and Van Dijk 259)

(3) Four or more authors.

List all four authors or give only the last name of the first author followed by *et al*.

It is most important to help students recover their self-confidence and courage as well as stimulate their interest in learning. In that way, the mental barrier can be cleared away and an interest in learning developed. Thus, the students' mind-set can be improved (Chen, et al. , 7).

The idea behind "Grave's Model" is not really to dissociate writing entirely from the written product and to merely lead students through various stages of the writing process but " to construct process-oriented writing instruction that will affect performance" (Freedman et al. , 13).

(4) Authors with the same last name.

Include the first initial in subsequent references. If the first initials are identical, we should spell out the first names. When the two authors are father and son, with the son designated as Jr. , we include the designation Jr. in the reference, preceded by a comma.

Helen C. White's The Mysticism of William Blake (H. White 75)

That book chronicles visionary experiences in early modern Spain (Christian, Jr.)

(5) Corporate author.

For a corporate author, we use the name of the organization (if the name is long, give a shortened form) in place of the name of the author.

It was apparent that the American health care system needed "to be fixed and perhaps radically modified" (Public Agenda Foundation 4)

(6) Author unknown.

For a work listed only by title in your list of works cited, if you do not use the complete title in a signal phrase, use the title in parentheses, shortening it to two or three words. Titles of books are underlined or italicized, titles of articles and other short works are put in quotation marks.

An Wordsworth critic once argued that his poems were too emotional ("Wordsworth Is A Loser" 100).

Before assuming that a web source has no author, do some detective work. Often the author's name is available but is hard to find. For example, it may appear at the end of the source, in tiny print. Or it may appear on another page of the site, such as the home page.

(7) Page number unknown.

You may omit the page number if a work lacks page numbers, as is the case with many web sources.

While word-processing makes writing and revising an easier, more satisfying experience for learners, there is no clear evidence that it actually improves students' writing (Pennington).

(8) Multiple citations by the same author.

Mention the title of the work in the signal phrase or include a shortened version of the title in the parentheses. Titles of articles and other short works are placed in quotation marks; titles of books are underlined or italicized.

Lightenor has argued that computers are not useful tools for small children ("Too Soon" 38), though he has acknowledged that early exposure to computer games does lead to better small motor skill development ("Hand-Eye Development" 17).

Or: Computers are not useful tools for small children (Lightenor, "Too Soon" 38), though he has acknowledged that early exposure to computer games does lead to better small motor skill development ("Hand-Eye Development" 17).

Or: Lightenor has argued that computers are not useful tools for small children, though he has acknowledged that early exposure to computer games does lead to better small motor skill development ("Too Soon" 38 and "Hand-Eye Development" 17).

Shaughnessy points out that "the beginning writer does not know how writers behave" (*errors* 79).

(9) Multiple citations by different author.

To cite more than one source, separate the citations with a semicolon.

The dangers of mountain lions to humans have been well documented (Rychnovsky 40; Seidensticker 114; Williams 30).

(10) Material cited in another source.

When a writer's or a speaker's quoted words appear in a source written by someone else, begin the citation with the abbreviation "qtd. in". The author and title of the source you actually consulted appear in the list of works cited.

Samuel Johnson admitted that Edmund Burke was an "extraordinary man" (qtd. in Broswell 2: 450).

You are advised to use this kind of indirect sources as little as possible. Relying too much on the secondary sources will undermine the credibility of your paper.

(11) Literary works.

Literary works can be found in numerous editions, your in-text citation usually consists of a page number from the edition you consulted. However, you should provide enough information as possible as you can—such as a section or chapter number, introduced with a semicolon and the appropriate abbreviation, after the page number so that our reader can locate the passage in another edition.

Margery Kempe relates the details of her journey to Constance with pilgrims headed for Jerusalem (96-98; bk. 1, chap. 26).

For drama and poetry, cite the work by act, scene, line, or section instead of the page number. Use Arabic numerals, and separate the numbers with periods.

What's in a name? That which we call a rose, by any other name would smell as sweet (2.2.23).

Many literary works, such as most short stories and many novels and plays, do not have parts or line numbers that you can refer to. In such cases, simply cite the page number.

3.5.2 Format of Works Cited

The list of sources, usually with the heading Works Cited appears at the end of the paper, starting on a new continuous page. Works Cited is sometimes referred to as References. Both terms mean the same thing—an alphabetical list of works you have cited or made reference to in the text. The title Works Cited is generally used when citing sources using MLA style, while References is used when citing sources using APA Style.

Place the title Works Cited in the center, about 2.5cm from the top of the page, and with a double-space from the first entry. We began each entry flush with the left margin, and if an entry runs more than one line, we indent the subsequent line or lines five spaces from the left margin.

The list of sources in APA style, usually with the heading References has the same location as the Works Cited in MLA style. But the entries in APA style are arranged differently. Moreover, by comparing the basic entries of MLA with that of APA, we can find the different orders and formats between two styles.

1) Entries for books in MLA style

① Author's last name and first name (and initial of the second name).

② Title of the book.

③ City or state of publication.

④ Name of the publisher.

⑤ Date of publication.

2) Entries for books in APA style

① Author's last name and initial of the first name (and the second name).

② Date of publication.

③ Title of the book (only the first word of the title and subtitle and proper names are capitalized).

④ City or state of publication.

⑤ Name of the publisher.

The CM style follows the note-bibliography system that gives much attention to the citations or footnotes and endnotes. The bibliography entries also provide the information of the author, title and facts of publication. The difference lies in that they refer to the complete work rather than a specific passage. So, they do not include page numbers. If they do when for an article, they list the inclusive pages of the entire article rather than the specific pages from which material was selected for citations. Moreover, they begin with the last name of the author or the first word of the title for the convenience of an alphabetical list of sources.

Here are the examples for each style.

Example of MLA   Tan, Amy. *The Bonesetter's Daughter*. New York: Putnam, 2001.

Example of APA   Baddeley, A. D. (1999). *Essentials of human memory*. Hove, England: Psychology Press.

Example of CM   Kizza, Joseph Migga. *Computer Network Security and Cyberethics*. Jefferson, N. C: McFarland, 2002.

The following are examples of entry forms for different sources in MLA style: books, articles, types of electronic media, and some other materials.

1) Entries for Books

(1) The title and subtitle.

① Works in an anthology.

Give the elements in the order as the following example.

Desai, Anita. "Scholar and Gypsy." *The Oxford Book of Travel Stories*. Ed. Patricia Craig. Oxford: Oxford UP, 1996. 251-273.

② Edition other than the first.

If you are citing an edition other than the first, include the number of the edition after the title (or after the names of any translators or editors that appear after the title): 2nd, 3rd, and so on.

Auletta, Ken. The Underclass. 2nd ed. Woodstock, NY: Overlook, 2000.

③ Multivolume work.

If you use more than one volume in a multivolume work, you need to include the total number of volumes before the city and publisher, using the abbreviation "vols."

Wellek, Rene. A History of Modern Criticism. 1750—1950. New Haven: Yale UP, 1955—1992. 8vols.

If your paper cites only one of the volumes, give the volume number before the city and publisher and publication information of the one we used.

Wellek, Rene. A History of Modern Criticism. 1750—1950. Vol. 8. New Haven: Yale UP, 1992.

④ Books in a series.

When the title page indicates that a book is part of a series, we need to give the series name and number, neither underlined nor enclosed in quotation marks, before the city of publication.

Malena Anne. *The Dynamics of Identity in Francophone Caribbean Narrative*. Francophone Cultures and lists. Ser. 24. New York: lang, 1998.

⑤ Encyclopedia or dictionary entry.

When an encyclopedia or dictionary is well known, simply list the author of the entry (if there is one), the title of the entry, the title of the reference work, the edition number (if any), and the date of the edition.

"Sonata." *The American Heritage Dictionary of the English Language*. 4th ed. 2000.

Brasingly, C. Reginald. "Birth Order." *Encyclopedia of Psychology*. Ed. Raymond J. Corsini, New York: Wiley, 1984.

⑥ Republished book.

After the title of the book, cite the original publication date, followed by the current publication information. If the republished book contains new material, such as an Introduction or Afterword, include information about the new material after the original date.

Hughes, Langston. *Black Misery*. 1969. Afterword Robert O'meally. New York: Oxford UP, 2000.

⑦ Foreword, introduction, preface, or afterword.

Begin with the author of the foreword or other book part, followed by the name of that part. Then give the title of the book; the author of the book, preceded by the word "by"; and the editor of the book (if any). After the publication information, give the page numbers of the part of the book being cited.

Hamill, Pete. Introduction. *The Brooklyn Reader: Thirty Writers Celebrate America's Favorite Borough*. Ed. Andrea Wyatt Sexton and Alice Leccese Powers. New York: Harmony, 1994. xi-xiv.

If the foreword, introduction, preface, or afterword has a title, include it immediately after the author's name enclosed in quotation marks.

Doody, Margaret Anne. "In Search of the Ancient Novel." Introduction. *The True Story of the Novel*. New Brunswick: Rutgers UP, 1996. 1-11.

⑧ Books in Chinese.

If you quote from a book written in Chinese, write the author's name in pinyin followed by the Chinese characters and a period. For the title of the book, write it in this order: pinyin, the Chinese characters, and the English translation in parentheses, followed by a period. You do not need to give the Chinese characters for the city in which the book is published and for the name of the publisher.

Liu Jianbo 刘浒波. *Nanfang Shiluo de Shijie: Fu Ke Na Xiaoshuo Yanjiu* 南方失落的世界——福克纳小说研究 (The Fallen World in the South: A Study of Faulkner's Novels). Chongqing: Southwest China Normal University Press, 1999.

⑨ Publisher's imprint.

If the book is part of an imprint — a name given to a group of books by the publisher, the name of the imprint is linked by a hyphen to the name of the publisher.

Truan, Barry. *Acoustic Communication*. Westport: Ablex-Greenwood, 2000.

(2) The place of publication, the publisher, and the date.

Take the information about the book from its title page and copyright page. Use a short form of the publisher's name; omit terms such as Press, Inc. and Co., except when naming university presses (Harvard UP, for example). If the copyright page lists more than one date, use the most recent one.

① Book with multiple publishers.

As part of the publication information, we put a semicolon between the names of the publishers.

Shelley, Percy Bysshe. *Selected Poems*. Ed. Timothy Webb. London: Dent; Totowa: Rowman, 1977.

② Book without stated publication information or pagination.

When the cited book does not indicate the publisher, the city or date of publication, we may, on the one hand, supply the missing information, using brackets to show that it comes from some other sources; on the other hand, we use a series of abbreviations for the information we cannot find: n. p. (no place/ no publisher), n. d. (no date of publication), and n. pag. (no pagination).

Sendak, Maurice. *Where the Wild Things Are*. New York: Harper, 1963. n. pag.

2) Entries for articles

The entry for an article in the works-cited list, like that for a book, has three main items: author's name, title of the article, and publication information.

(1) Article in a magazine.

For a weekly magazine, we give the complete date (beginning with the day and abbreviating the month except May, June, and July). For a monthly magazine, we give the month and year. For both, we do not give the volume and issue number. If it is an anonymous article, we begin the entry with the title.

Kaplan, Robert D. " History Moving North. " *Atlantic Monthly* Feb. 1997: 21.

(2) Article in a newspaper.

List the following elements, in order, separated by periods: the author's name, the title of the article in quotation marks, the name of the newspaper, the date, and the page number including the section letter. If the article is not printed on consecutive pages, use a plus sign "+" after the page number.

Manning, Anita. "Curriculum Battles from Left and Right." *USA Today* 2 Mar. 1994: D5.

(3) Article in a scholarly journal.

Many scholarly journals continue page numbers throughout the year instead of beginning each issue with page 1; at the end of the year, the issues are collected in a volume. If each issue of the journal begins with page 1, we need to indicate the number of the issue. After the volume number, put a period and the issue number. When a journal is numbered by issue rather than by volume, treat the issue number as the volume number.

Gardner, Thomas. " An Interview with Jorie Graham. " *Denver Quarterly* 26. 4 (1992): 79-104.

Nwezeh, C. E. " The Comparative Approach to Modern African Literature. " *Yearbook of General and Comparative Literature* 28 (1979): 22-30.

(4) Article in an editorial.

Begin with the author's name if it is a signed editorial, but with the title if it is not. We label it with "Editorial" and conclude it with some necessary publication information.

"Potomac Yard Decision. " Editorial. *Washington Post* 16 Oct. 1992: A24.

(5) Article in a review.

Name the reviewer and the title of the review, if any, followed by the words " Rev. of" and the title and author or director of the work reviewed, and the facts of publication.

Moore, Walter. " Great Physicist, Great Guy. " Rev. of *Genius*: *The life and Science of Richard Feynman*, by James Gleick. *New York Times Book Review* 11 Oct. 1992:3.

Denby, David. "On the Battlefield. " Rev. of *The Hurricane*, dir. Norman Jewison. *New Yorker* 10 Jan. 2000: 90-92.

3) Entries for electronic media

In contrast with print sources, electronic media, so far, lack agreed-on means of organizing works. The minimum information for an electronic source includes: the author, if any; the title of the section you used, in quotation marks; the title of the entire source, underlined; volume or issue number; year or date of publication in parentheses; number of pages if applicable; a description of the medium (CD-ROM, diskette, etc.); the name of the computer network or vendor and, if it is not well known, an address preceded by the word "available"; the date of electronic publication; if necessary for your purpose, the equipment required to run it; and, in the case of on-line or e-mail materials, the date you accessed the source. You may supply the electronic address or path at the end of the entry. Usually, some of these elements will not apply or will be unavailable, cite whatever we do have.

(1) Work from a web site.

List the following elements in order: author's name (if there is no author, begin with the title); title of the work in quotation marks; title of the site italicized; date of publication or last update; sponsor of the site (if any); date you accessed the source; the URL in angle brackets (< >) followed by a period.

Shiva, Vandana. "Bioethics: A Third World Issue." *Nativeweb*. 15 Sept. 2001<http://www.*nativeweb*.org/pages/legal/shiva.html>.

(2) Work from online book.

Give as much publication information as is available, followed by the date of access and the URL.

Barsky, Robert F. *Noam Chomsky: A life of Dissent*. Cambridge: MTP, 1997. 8 May 1998 <http://mitpress.mit.edu/e-books/chomsky/>.

If a part of an online book is cited, place the part title before the book's title. If the part is a short work such as a poem or an essay, put its title in quotation marks. If the part is an introduction, a preface, or other division of the book, do not use quotation marks.

Adams, Henry. "Diplomacy." *The Education of Henry Adams*. Boston: Houghton, 1918. *Bartleby.com: Great Books Online*. 1999. 17 Feb. 2003 <http://bartley.com/159/8.html>.

(3) Work from online journal.

When citing online articles, follow the guidelines for printed articles, giving whatever information is available in the online source. End the citation with the date of access and the URL.

Tully, R. Brent, et al. " Global Extinction in Spiral Galaxies." *Astronomical Journal* 115.6 (1998). 27 June 1998<http://www.jouranls.uchicago.edu/AJ? journal/issues/vll5n6/980002/980002.html>.

(4) Work from CD-ROM.

Treat the work from CD-ROM as you would as any other sources, but name the medium before the publication information.

"Pimpernel." *The American Heritage Dictionary of the English Language*. 4th ed. CD-ROM. Boston Houghton, 2000.

(5) Work from e-mail.

To cite an e-mail, begin with the writer's name and the subject line. Then write "E-mail to" followed by the name of the recipient. End with the date of the message.

Boyle, Anthony T. " Re: Utopia." E-mail to Daniel J. Cahill. 21 June 1998.

4) Entries for some other materials

(1) Government publication.

Begin the entry with the government agency if you do not know the writer of the document. The document's author, editor, or compiler may either begin the entry or, if the agency comes first, follow the title and the word "By" or abbreviation "Ed." or "Comp". If the government documents published online, give as much publication information as is available and end your citation with the date of access and the URL.

Australian Bureau of Statistics. *Social Trends in Australia* 2004. Canberra, 2004.

United States. Dept. of Transportation. Natl. Highway Traffic Safety Administration. *An investigation of the Safety Implications of Wireless Communications in Vehicles*. Nov. 1999. 20 May 2001<http://www.nhtsa.dot.gov/people/injury/research/wireless>.

(2) Pamphlet.

Treat a pamphlet as a book.

Hogarth, P.J. The Biology of Mangroves. Oxford: Oxford University Press, 1999.

(3) Dissertation.

A published dissertation is documented as a book, specially marked with Diss. before the publication facts. If the dissertation has not been published yet, use quotation marks to enclose the title, and then Diss. and the name of the degree-granting university to label it.

Moskop, William W. *The Prudent Politician: An Extension of Aristotle's Ethical Theory*. Diss. George Washington U,1984. Ann Ardor: UMI, 1985. 85-13289.

Byrne, Maritza Ivonne. "Self-talk and Test Anxiety." Diss. Monash University, Melbourne, 1966.

(4) Published Conference Papers.

Treat published conference proceedings as a book, adding information about the conference after the title. For an unpublished paper, the details are common.

Mick. *The Role of Economics in Natural Heritage Decision Making*. Proc. of the International Society for Ecological Economics Conf., 4 July 2000. Canberra: Australian Heritage Commission, 2001.

3.6 Acknowledgements

The acknowledgements section contains expressions of appreciation for assistance and guidance. Acknowledgements should be expressed simply and tactfully. Permissions that you have obtained for quotations may be presented in the acknowledgments or on the copyright page. When permissions are granted as a special favor, they are best placed in the acknowledgments.

You should write the advisor's name in the beginning, and then the name of those who gave you assistance, and helped you technically and financially.

The following is an example, you could make use of it as a guide.

I would like to acknowledge and extend my heartfelt gratitude to the following persons who have made the completion of this "Lecture Notes" possible.

Our Dear, DR. _____ (name of person), for her vital encouragement and support.

_____ (name), for her understanding and assistance.

_____ (name), Chair, Department of Pharmacy for the constant reminders and much needed motivation.

_____ (name)... for the help and inspiration he extended.

All _____ (name of department) faculty members and Staff.

The _____ (other contributors), for assisting in the collection of the topics for the chapters.

Most especially to my family and friends.

And to God, who made all things possible.

More examples are provided below.

Acknowledgements 1

I thank my committee for their help with this thesis. I would also like to thank the following important people in my life: my parents for giving me the opportunity to pursue my dreams; my sister, Marsha, for always being there to listen, offer support and make me smile; my brother, Manoj, for his prayers and support; Catherine Duran for being such an incredible friend throughout this process; Spike and Bonnie for their unconditional love, and most importantly, I thank ..., for his patience, support and encouragement. Thank you all.

Acknowledgements 2

I would like to express my gratitude to my supervisor Mr. ... for his supervision of my paper. I must also extend my gratitude to all the Professor..., lecturers of the MBA program whose dedication to teaching enlightened our lifelong pursuit for knowledge.

Thanks to all my diligent and brilliant colleagues in the MBA program and those supported me during my research.

A special word of thanks to my family for their unwavering support.

Acknowledgements 3

Over the years, many colleagues in both the academic and business worlds have provided us with valuable insights into the management and marketing of services, through their writings and in conference or seminar discussions. We have also benefited enormously from in-class and after-class discussions with MBA and executive program participants.

We are pleased to acknowledge the insightful and helpful comments of our editorial advisory board: ... We also express gratitude to ... for their reviews of the first edition. We are grateful, too, to the many instructors who adopted the book, and suggested improvements to this new edition. They challenged our thinking and, through their critiques and suggestions, encouraged us to include many substantial changes.

Although it's impossible to mention everyone who has influenced our thinking over the years, we particularly want to express our appreciation to the following individuals:...

Acknowledgements 4

I would like to convey my sincere thanks to my family and friends who gave me a lot of support, assistance and encouragement throughout the year. My special thanks should be given to ..., my advisor, who has dedicated a lot of his time and patience to me. Without his encouragement I don't think I can accomplish this difficult task by my own.

Chapter 4　Optional

4.1　A Thesis on English Education

A Survey of Language Learning Strategies of English Majors

Abstract

   This thesis investigates how well the junior English majors in a science university make use of language learning strategies automatically, whether students' achievements is related to using language learning strategies properly or not, and whether students need teachers' instructions of language learning strategies or not. 55 students from Wuhan Institute of Technology were intentionally chosen to attend a quantitative survey of a close-ended questionnaire, and meanwhile, two students were chosen to participate in an interview—one is an excellent student and the other is a poor student. Findings prove that generally the learners basically have command of language learning strategies; more than half of the students can apply management strategies, while more than half of the students are not able to use method strategies; students' TEM-4 scores are in proportion to how well they use language learning strategies. At the end of the paper, some suggestions are put forward to help students develop learning strategies and improve learning efficiency.

   Key words: language learning strategies, questionnaire, conversation, learning efficiency

摘 要

本文在国内外对外语学习策略研究的基础之上,通过问卷和座谈两种形式调查了理工科大学英语专业学生在课外自主使用学习策略的现状,进而了解优秀生和学困生运用学习策略与学习效果的关系及学生是否需要老师在学习策略方面给些建议。来自武汉工程大学的 55 名学生参与了问卷调查。调查者还从问卷中选出两个学生(一个优秀生和一个学困生)进行了座谈。通过对问卷调查结果和座谈的分析,发现学生们总体上基本能够运用学习策略,对于管理策略,超过半数的人能够较好运用,但有超过半数的人不善于运用方法策略,结果表明学生的专业英语四级考试成绩与运用学习策略的好坏成正比。座谈后鉴于学生们需要教师提供些学习策略,本文就此种情况提出了一些建议。

关键词:学习策略,问卷,座谈,学习效果

Contents

Abstract ……………………………………………………………………… (Ⅰ)

摘要 …………………………………………………………………………… (Ⅱ)

1 Introduction ………………………………………………………………… (1)

   1.1 The Definition of Language Learning Strategies ………………… (1)

   1.2 The Classification of Language Learning Strategies ……………… (2)

   1.3 Literature Review ……………………………………………………… (3)

   1.4 The Purpose of This Paper …………………………………………… (4)

2 Research Methods …………………………………………………………… (5)

   2.1 Research Participants ………………………………………………… (5)

   2.2 Research Instruments ………………………………………………… (6)

      2.2.1 Questionnaire …………………………………………………… (6)

      2.2.2 Objectives of the Interview …………………………………… (6)

3 Data Collecting and Processing …………………………………………… (7)

   3.1 Questionnaire Data Collection ………………………………………… (7)

   3.2 Interview Data Collection ……………………………………………… (7)

4 Results and Discussion ……………………………………………………… (9)

   4.1 Results of the Questionnaire and Discussion ……………………… (9)

   4.2 Results of the Interview and Discussion …………………………… (11)

   4.3 Suggestions …………………………………………………………… (13)

5 Conclusion …………………………………………………………………… (14)

Bibliography …………………………………………………………………… (15)

Appendix: Language Learning Strategy Questionnaire …………………… (16)

1 Introduction

1.1 The Definition of Language Learning Strategies

Within foreign language education, a number of definitions of language learning strategies have been given by key figures in this field.

Early on, Tarone (1983) defined learning strategies as "an attempt to develop linguistic and sociolinguistic competence in the target language—to incorporate these into one's interlingua competence".

Weinstein and Mayer (1986) defined learning strategies broadly as "behaviors and thoughts that a learner engages in during learning which intend to influence the learner's process".

Rubin (1987) later wrote that learning strategies "are strategies which contribute to the development of the language system which the learner constructs and influences learning directly".

Later Mayer (1988) more specially defined learning strategies as "behaviors of a learner that are intended to influence how the learner processes information". The early definitions from the education literature reflect the roots of learning strategies in cognitive science, with its essential assumption that human beings process information and that learning involves such information processing.

In their seminal study, O'Malley and Chamot (1990) defined learning strategies as "the special thoughts or behaviors that individuals use to help them comprehend, learn, or retain new information".

Finally, Oxford (1992—1993) provides special examples of language learning strategies and a helpful definition: language learning strategies—specific actions, behaviors, steps, or techniques that students (often intentionally) use to improve their process in developing language skills. These strategies can facilitate the internalization, storage, retrieval, or use of the new language. Strategies are tools for the self-directed involvement necessary for developing communicative ability.

1.2 The Classification of Language Learning Strategies

Different scholars lay their own stress on defining learning strategies; therefore, there are a variety of classifications of learning strategies. Cohen (1987) divides learning strategies into two groups: language learning strategies and language using strategies. The former includes strategies for identifying the material that needs to be learned, distinguishing it from other materials, grouping it for easier learning, memorizing it when natural acquisition is impossible and so on. The latter, more specially, includes four subsets of strategies: retrieval strategies, rehearsal strategies, cover strategies and communication strategies.

Rubin (1987) prefers to use the term "learner strategies" to mean "learning strategies". She recognizes three major types of learner strategies based on reception production model. Learning strategies refer to the strategies that may directly affect learning, which can be further divided into "cognitive strategies which are concerned with language production, enabling learner to keep the communication going despite their limitation in knowledge and competence and social strategies that concern about the ways in which learner's select interact with other learners and native speakers".

Based on the information-processing model, O'Mally and Chamot (1985) recognize three major types of strategies. They are met-cognitive strategies, cognitive strategies and social-affective strategies.

Oxford (1990) emphasizes the effect that learning strategies have on the learning process, groups learning strategies into two major categories: direct strategies and indirect strategies. Language learning strategies that directly involve the target language learning through focusing, planning, evaluating, controlling anxiety, increasing cooperation and other means are called indirect strategies.

Stern's (1992) classification of language learning strategies is composed of five parts: management and planning strategies, cognitive strategies, communicative-experimental strategies, interpersonal strategies, affective strategies.

Wen Qiufang (1993) stresses on two aspects: one is the relationship between learning strategies and learning process, the other is the relationship between learning strategies and learning materials. She divides learning strategies system into three parts: concepts of language learning strategies, management strategies and language learning strategies.

Their definitions are as follows.

Concepts of language learning strategies: students' recognition of how to study English well. Management strategies: in order to arrange and organize their language learning, they make a series of measures, such as making a plan, estimating progress and moderate emotion. These strategies usually have nothing to do with language learning materials.

Method strategies: these strategies are directly related to English language learning materials. The ways to practice listening, speaking, reading, writing and studying grammar and intonations are included.

Wen Qiufang's classification is based on western classification of learning strategies. Moreover, her classification mainly concerns about learning settings in China. Therefore, with the classification provided by Wen Qiufang, Chinese learners may perceive learning strategies in a more direct way and they are likely to select the strategies they need with greater assurance and confidence. Therefore, this paper will choose this classification for investigation.

1.3 Literature Review

The development of psycholinguistics in the 1960s has directed considerable attention to the process of language acquisition, both mother tongue and second language. In the case of second language learning, error analysis has been used as a basis for theorizing on the strategies used by the learner that has resulted in the deviant forms in the surface structure of his utterances in the target language. The rationale behind this approach lies in the belief that a learner's systematic errors provide evidence of how language is learnt and "what strategies or procedure the learner is employing in his discovery of language" (Cord, 1976).

Since the 1960s, the study of learner strategies has received more and more attention in the field of English learning and teaching, and a great deal has been discovered about the learning process and learner strategies.

In most of the researches on language learning strategies, the primary concern has been on "identifying what good language learners report they do to learn a second or foreign language, or, in some cases, are observed doing while learning a second or foreign language"(Rubin and Wenden, 1987). Rubin initiates research focusing on the strategies of successful learners and stated that such strategies could be made available to less successful learners (Rubin, 1987). He classifies strategies in terms of processes contributing directly and indirectly to language learning (Rubin, 1987). Wong-Fillmore (1982—1985) identifies social strategies used by successful language learners. Tarone (1980) studies the communication strategies of language learners. Research conducted by Naiman, et al. (1978) focuses on personality traits, cognitive styles and strategies that are critical to successful language learning. Bialystok's report (1979) shows the effects of the use of two functional strategies—inference and functional practicing, and two formal strategies—a study that will give English teachers valuable information on how their students process information, plan and select the most suitable strategies to understand or solve a problem. As a result, teachers will be able to help their students become better language learners by training them in using appropriate strategies. The study contributes to this field by giving information on the strategies that Chinese learners use and how they use the strategies to understand information.

In China, researches on language learning strategies have been increasing in recent years. Among them, the following are worth mentioning: Huang Xiaohua first investigates learning strategies for oral communication in 1984; Wu Yian and Liu Runqing, et al. (1993) investigate the psychological and social-psychological factors of English learning; Wen Qiufang (1995) compares different learning strategies employed by successful learners and unsuccessful learners and (1996) systematically studied English learning strategies in a book entitled *English Learning Strategies*.

1.4　The Purpose of This Paper

This study, with the intention of surveying the situation of third-year English majors applying language learning strategies to their study, will focus on three research questions: ① how well the English majors in a science university make use of language learning strategies consciously; ② whether students' achievements is related to using language learning strategies or not; ③ whether students need teachers' instructions on language learning strategies or not.

2 Research Methods

2.1 Research Participants

   This study surveyed the third-year English majors from Wuhan Institute of Technology, a key science university in Hubei. As the participants of the research, the third-year English majors were chosen for the following three reasons: firstly, as they are juniors, they are more likely to experience a great deal of English learning difficulties or problems and have their own language learning strategies; secondly, since they all took part in TEM-4 and got different scores, the relationship between TEM-4 scores and language learning strategies can be investigated; thirdly, they are all from the same college which helps to avoid a subjective selection of subjects from the research.

   Based on the above reasons of the selection of participants, 55 third-year English majors from 3 different classes in school of foreign languages of Wuhan Institute of Technology responded to the questionnaire on April 22nd, 2007. 49 are females and the rest 6 are males. 48 of them passed TEM-4 test in April, 2005. All the subjects had learned English formally for six years in high schools and for three more years as university students. In this study, the samples are distributed in terms of gender, the scores of English course in their college entrance examination and academic records in TEM-4 as shown in Table 4-1.

Table 4-1

	Gender		English Scores (College Entrance Examination)［单位:分］				TEM-4	
	Male	Female	120—129	110—119	100—109	0—99	pass	fail
Frequency（人数）	6	49	23	25	5	2	48	7
Percent（百分比）	10.91	89.09	41.82	45.45	9.09	3.64	87.27	12.73

   From the above table, we know that the subjects have two distinctive characteristics. One is that the number of the female students greatly exceeds the number of the male students, which can be explained by the fact that female students are generally regarded by Chinese people as being more suitable to learn foreign languages because they can do better than male students. The other characteristic is that most students' (87.27%) English scores in their college entrance exam is over 110.

2.2 Research Instruments

2.2.1 Questionnaire

The questionnaire is composed of two parts. In the first part, personal information is presented. The second part which is about Wen Qiufang's language learning system, including concepts of language learning and methods of language learning, was administered to collect information on language learners' individual opinions and methods. The questionnaire contains 40 close-ended questions, and three choices were given to the first 10 questions (from 1 to 3 option attached by 1 to 3 points), five choices were given to the following 30 questions(from 1 to 5 option attached by 1 to 5 points). All the subjects were asked to choose one of the three or five options that best describe their own situations. Chinese, rather than English, is used to write the questionnaire to avoid possible misunderstanding or difficulties for the students.

Among 40 questions, questions 1~10 ask the subjects to make a self-assessment about their attitude toward some ideas on learning English; questions 11~20 try to find out whether they are able to use appropriate language learning strategies to manage their English study; questions 21~40 aim to examine their ability to use the language learning strategies to improve their English proficiency. The 40 questions are believed to have covered all the important information which is needed to answer the three research questions.

2.2.2 Objectives of the Interview

Two students were chosen as typical examples with three objectives. The first objective is to know more exactly about the differences between successful learners and unsuccessful learners using language learning strategies. The second objective is to find whether the excellent student is better at adopting learning strategies than the poor student. The third objective is that through this interview, the researcher wants to know whether students need correct instructions from their teachers to learn English well.

3 Data Collecting and Processing

3.1 Questionnaire Data Collection

Two teachers helped to distribute the questionnaires in their classes to the subjects. Before the two teachers went into their classrooms to have their lessons, the researcher explained to the subjects in great detail of the purpose of the research and what they should do when they answer the questionnaires. The teachers were asked to emphasize to the participants that they were required to answer the questionnaires with honesty. The two teachers also agreed to give the subjects enough time (at least 15 minutes) to complete the questionnaires. When returning the copies of the questionnaires to the researcher, all the two teachers said they had strictly followed the requirements.

3.2 Interview Data Collection

The researcher asked for help from supervisor Professor Miss Tu to choose two questionnaires' owners respectively. Then the researcher went to their dormitories and tried to seek for their cooperation. The researcher emphasized that the conversation would not affect the points of their final examination and their name will not be written in the paper. Consequently, they agreed to cooperate.

In the interview, the researcher asked the following questions.
(1) Could you tell me something about your family?
(2) Are you a arts student or a science student in high school?
(3) How many years have you studied English till now?
(4) Are you interested in English?
(5) How much time do you spend in studying English after class?
(6) Do you have any plan in learning English?
(7) How do you preview intensive English course, study it in class and review it?
(8) How do you practice your English listening skill?
(9) Do you read English newspaper, magazines or novels? If yes, how do you read them?
(10) Do you have a habit to keep diary or essay?
(11) What is your performance in your oral English classes?
(12) Do you practice your oral English after class?

(13) Have you ever reflected on your English study? If you find out your weaknesses, do you take measures to remedy them?

(14) In the four skills of listening, speaking, reading, writing, which is your strongest and which is your worst skill?

Questions (1) to (4) are designed to know the background of two students' families and their English study conditions. Then questions (5) to (7) are about the management strategies. Question (6) is on how they study intensive English course. The rest seven questions concern about the four skills: listening, speaking, reading and writing.

4 Results and Discussion

4.1 Results of the Questionnaire and Discussion

There are altogether 55 valid copies of the questionnaires which were processed to answer the research questions. The researcher spent half a week in processing the data collected from the 55 copies of the questionnaires. The processing job was carefully carried out and the result was checked for three times to ensure its correctness.

The language learning strategies automatically used by the third-year English majors are shown in Table 4-2.

Table 4-2

—	Language Learning Strategies(Total score is 180)		
	Excellent (144—180)	Good (108—144)	Poor (0—108)
Frequency	4	35	16
Percent	7.27	63.64	29.09

Table 4-2 shows clearly that most participants got scores between 108 and 144. It stands to reason that they are good at employing language learning strategies. The rest are ones who are poor at using learning strategies. Only 7.27% of the participants got scores more than 144. On the whole, most students apply learning strategies actively. However, there are few students who are excellent at using it.

At last, the information of the questionnaires was collected and sorted out for analyzing. The participants' attitude towards English learning is shown in Table 4-3.

Table 4-3　Concepts of language learning

—	Option 1 (单位:人次)	Percent (百分数)	Option 2 (单位:人次)	Percent (百分数)	Option 3 (单位:人次)	Percent (百分数)
Question 1	19	35.55	22	40	14	25.45
Question 2	2	3.64	1	1.82	52	94.54
Question 3	1	1.82	0	0.00	54	98.18
Question 4	1	1.82	5	9.09	49	89.09
Question 5	3	5.46	16	29.09	36	65.45
Question 6	1	1.82	7	12.73	47	85.45
Question 7	1	1.82	5	9.09	49	89.09
Question 8	4	7.27	23	41.82	28	50.91
Question 9	29	52.73	18	32.73	8	14.54
Question 10	28	50.91	20	36.36	7	12.73

From the above table some conclusions are drawn. For the first question (students who are good at English have talent in it), 22 students did not have clear idea. 19 students denied this opinion. Meanwhile, 14 students agreed on this opinion. Therefore, on the whole, more students regarded that talent plays a less important role than diligence does. When it comes to the next six questions, in other words, from question 2 to question 7, 55 students chose option 3. It signifies that a large number of students realized that proper plans for study and good English learning methods were important to English study. Question 8 is about whether reading English newspapers, magazines and novels is more useful than intensive reading course. 28 students chose positive answer, while the rest 23 students did not have clear idea. The last two questions are related to English thinking ability. More than half of the students thought that it was better to use English thinking before speaking and writing. However, when being asked whether a good command of English learning strategies is important for them, most students (52 subjects) answered "yes". Only one of them thought it was hard to decide and there are still two participants who answered "no".

Before the second part was analyzed, 55 copies of questionnaires were divided into two parts according to their TEM-4 scores. The first part contained 27 copies whose owners' TEM-4 scores are not over 65. And those students are considered as relatively poor students. The second part includes 28 copies, whose owners' TEM-4 scores are from 66 to 79. And they are regarded to be relatively excellent students. The second part of questionnaire on language learning strategies contains two kinds of strategies (management strategies and method strategies). When the researcher designed the questionnaire, every option was attached with points. The answers' total points included three ranks, that is, excellent, good, and poor. The excellent rank includes the points over 80% of the total points, and then points over 60% are regarded as the good rank. The poor rank includes the points under 60%. As to management strategies, from 40 points to 50 points is excellent, then from 30 points to 40 points is good and from 0 points to 30 points is poor. As to method strategies, from 80 points to 100 points is excellent, then from 60 points to 80 points is good and from 0 points to 60 points is poor.

The results are shown in the following tables—Table 4-4 and Table 4-5.

Table 4-4

TEM-4(单位：分)	Management strategies（单位：人次）			Percent(百分数)		
	Excellent (40—50)	Good (30—40)	Poor (0—30)	Excellent (40—50)	Good (30—40)	Poor (0—30)
Poor(0—65)	6	11	10	22.22	40.74	37.04
Excellent(66—79)	4	16	8	14.29	57.14	28.57

Table 4-5

TEM-4(单位:分)	Method strategies (单位:人次)			Percent(百分数)		
	Excellent (80—100)	Good (60—80)	Poor (0—60)	Excellent (80—100)	Good (60—80)	Poor (0—60)
Poor(0—65)	1	13	13	3.70	48.15	48.15
Excellent(66—79)	0	13	15	0.00	46.43	53.57

From Table 4-4, we can see that up to 71.43% (14.29%+57.14%) of the students, whose TEM-4 scores (from 66 to 79) are excellent and good at management strategies. And 62.96% (22.22%+40.74%) of the students whose TEM-4 scores are not over 65 are also excellent and good at management strategies. Therefore, both two kinds of students have good command of management strategies. And the different rate between excellent students (TEM-4 scores between 66 and 79) and relatively poor students (TEM-4 score between 0 and 65) is only 8.47%. From this result, it can be seen that the juniors are good at management strategies or at least they know how to arrange their study and excellent students are relatively better at using management strategies.

From Table 4-5, 53.57% of excellent students are poor at method strategies, while 48.15% of relatively poor students are poor at those strategies. It means that both excellent and poor students are weak in applying method strategies and it is interesting to find out that the poor students do a little better than excellent students in using method strategies. And the different rate between them is 5.42%. On the whole, combining two strategies together, we can understand that more excellent students are better at using strategies than poor students. The different rate is 3.69%.

4.2 Results of the Interview and Discussion

1. General comparison

The researcher compared the two students' questionnaires in four aspects. It is shown in the following Table 4-6. Student A represents the excellent student, and student B stands for poor students.

Table 4-6

—	Concepts of LLS	Management Strategies	Method Strategies	Total Point
Student A	27	39	68	134
Student B	22	22	40	84

From the above table, we can see their points of every aspect clearly. Student A has 5, 17, 28 points more than student B respectively in concepts of language learning strategies, management strategies and method strategies. The total different points between them is 50. Although student B also has a positive concept in using language learning strategies, she does use few language learning strategies. So she is poor at studying English and her TEM-4 score is 52. However, student A is good at using language learning strategies and her TEM-4 score is 72.

2. Their family background

After our conversation, the researcher wrote down the notes of what they said. Student A is from Xiaogan city of Hubei province and her parents are peasants who couldn't help her in English study. Student B is from Liuzhou city in Guangxi province and her parents are businessmen. They had no time to help her study English.

3. Their effort in the learning process

Student A is always willing to invest her time and energy in English learning. She worked harder and had done many exercises in and out of class. During her leisure time, she liked listening to English tapes, watching English films, or reading English materials. She tended to do more than student B and than what her teacher assigned. What is more, she could sustain her effort and devote energy to it during the whole learning process. However, student B spent nearly no time in learning English after class.

4. Their plans on English study

Usually on her mind, student A had a plan to arrange her English study. However, she did not have a plan in detail. As to the four skills, she was good at reading but poor at listening and speaking. Occasionally, she communicated with other students about language learning strategies and reflected on her study, then tried her best to make a progress. Student B hardly did that.

5. Their determination to study English

Student A had a strong will to learn English well. She usually encouraged herself when encountering problems or difficulties in the process of study. On the contrary, student B said, "When I entered our college, I found that students from Hubei province were good at study. Gradually I could not catch up with them. Once in a while, I made up my mind to study, but did not persist in it. So at last, I gave up study."

6. Whether they want instructions from teachers

Student B participated in a large number of activities. She had no more time to study and also had no strategies to study. From the bottom of her heart, she wanted to study well, but she could not find a good study method that she could persist in. She desired to be forced to study. The researcher told her that study in college is different from that in high school or middle school. She said, "I know I should study by myself, but the poor students like me really need teachers to teach us some strategies." So for the students who couldn't form their own strategies, teachers' advice would be useful.

7. Whether students' achievements are related to using language learning strategies properly

Good learners, as we can notice in our research, often make remarkable achievements. Student A got a high point in TEM-4 while student B did not pass it.

From the questionnaires' results and the discussion, we can see that excellent students are relatively better at applying learning strategies. From the interview, it comes out that students A (excellent student) got higher point than student B (poor student) in TEM-4. Therefore, students' TEM-4 scores are in proportion to how well they use language learning strategies.

4.3 Suggestions

After the interview, when the researcher asked the two students whether it is necessary that teachers give them some instructions about how to use language learning strategies, their answer was "yes". So some suggestions were put forward by the writer of this paper.

(1) Teachers should help students to establish a correct attitude towards English learning.

Students' attitude to study and use language learning strategies is determined by their concepts. Teachers should make them understand the fact that learning foreign language is a complex process, but it can be controlled by learners themselves. It is helpful to use language learning strategies appropriately in English study. The most important thing of learning English is working hard and persisting in it.

(2) During the teaching process, teachers should introduce some strategies and consolidate them in use.

In class, teachers could introduce some useful language learning strategies to students and strictly train students to use them. Although some students have some strategies, they do not know how to use them in their study. What is worse, when they confront difficulties or problems, they do not change their strategies but use the invalid strategies again and again. Accordingly, teachers had better teach students to adopt strategies.

(3) Teachers should communicate with students regularly and know their problems or difficulties and help them to solve problems or solve problems by themselves.

A large number of students are accustomed to relying on teachers' instillation. They are lack of the ability to solve problems and difficulties in study. In college, students have few chances to meet their teachers. If students encounter problems and difficulties which always can not be solved promptly, and put them aside time and time again, they would have bigger problems. Besides, different students have different characters and study habits, only teachers know their exact situation and can help students out. Although in today's society, it is advocated that students should control their own study consciously, it does not mean that they do not need teachers' help.

5 Conclusion

Although the relationship between language learning strategies and students' achievements is complex, if one usually uses a great number of strategies, he or she will get high points in tests. Language learning strategies are the essential skills in English study, and it is a component of life-long education, so its importance stands on reason.

This paper has found out that many third-year English majors are able to use strategies to overcome the difficulties or problems in their study and they get satisfactory learning results. However, some poor students can not do that or they know few strategies.

The students' TEM-4 scores are in proportion to how well they use language learning strategies.

Due to the limitations of the present study, the research calls for further studies on language learning strategy instructions of English majors to be conducted both by researchers and teachers in college.

Firstly, the future studies should include English majors from more grades and more schools. Although the term "Chinese English majors" is used to label one general type of EFL learners in China, the truth is that all English majors do not belong to a uniform group. In fact, because they are from different grades and different places in China, the so-called "English majors" consist of different students with different English learning characters, different English learning settings and other different elements which may influence their English study. For this reason, the future studies should include a variety of English majors from different kinds of different grades as their subjects.

Secondly, the studies on language learning strategies or language learning strategy instructions in the Chinese context are in urgent need of a new strategy inventory for language learning, which should be specially designed for all Chinese EFL learners different from Oxford's SILL (1990). Therefore, some future studies can be launched for the purpose of working out a scientific and comprehensive strategy inventory, which can fit both the Chinese EFL context and the Chinese EFL learners.

Finally, some future studies should aim to improve the language learning strategy instructions of the Chinese English majors. These studies should provide more valuable research findings in relation to all the important aspects of strategy instructions. In other words, these studies should be able to contribute directly to the improvement of their language learning efficiency of all English majors in China.

Bibliography

[1] COHEN A D. Strategies in learning and using a second language[M]. 北京:外语教学与研究出版社,2000.

[2] HARMER J. How to teach English[M]. 北京:外语教学与研究出版社,2000.

[3] NUNAN D. The learner-centered curriculum: a study in second language teaching[M]. 上海:上海外语教育出版社,2001.

[4] TARONE E,YULE G. Focus on the language learner[M]. 上海:上海外语教育出版社,2000.

[5] 文秋芳.英语学习策略论[M].上海:上海外语教育出版社,1996.

Appendix

Language Learning Strategy Questionnaire

英语学习策略调查

亲爱的同学：

你好！为了真实全面地了解我校英语专业学生的英语学习现状，请你回答这份调查问卷。你的回答只反映你对相关问题的基本看法和认识，没有对错之分。你真诚的合作是我们做好研究的基础和保证，也是对我们研究的支持和鼓励。谢谢！

万丽　涂朝莲
2010 年 4 月

第一部分　个人简况

1. 你的性别_____
2. 你现在所在的年级和班级_____
3. 你高考的英语成绩_____分
4. 你是否已经通过英语专业四级考试_____　A. 是　B. 否
5. 你的英语专业四级考试成绩是_____分
6. 你课外每星期花大约多少时间学习英语？_____小时

第二部分　调查项目

（一）你对英语学习的看法（学习策略系统之观念）

下面是人们对英语学习的一些看法，这些看法没有对错之分，请大家根据每个数字所代表的含义选出其中一个写在句子的开头，所选择的选项一定要能如实代表你自己的看法。

1 = 我不同意这个看法
2 = 对这个看法我没有明确的答案
3 = 我同意这个看法

1. _____英语学得好的人具有学习英语的天分。
2. _____选择有效的学习方法对学好英语很重要。
3. _____学习英语需要下工夫。
4. _____有明确的长期或短期的目标对学好英语很重要。
5. _____要学好英语，后天的努力比先天的能力更重要。
6. _____经常反思自己的学习方法是否有效对学习英语非常重要。
7. _____反复模仿好的录音对练好语音语调很重要。
8. _____要学好英语，阅读英文报纸、杂志、小说等比精读更重要。
9. _____要想写出好的英语作文，最好的方法是先用中文组织好想写的内容。
10. _____说英语时，最好先用中文想好要说的内容。

（二）你学习英语的做法（学习策略系统之方法）

下面是人们常用的学习策略，请根据数字所代表的意思，选择其中的一个填在句子的开头，所选择的选项一定要能如实代表你自己的看法。请记住在填写时，要根据自己的实际做法而不是你的想法或其他人的做法。

1＝这种做法完全或几乎完全不适合我的情况
2＝这种做法通常不适合我的情况
3＝这种做法有时适合我的情况
4＝这种做法通常适合我的情况
5＝这种做法完全或几乎完全适合我的情况

管理策略：

11. _____ 除了老师布置的作业外，我有自己的英语学习计划。
12. _____ 为了使自己有足够的时间学习英语，我能很好地安排自己的学习日程。
13. _____ 我对改进自己的英语学习有明确的要求。
14. _____ 我评价自己学习英语进步的情况，从而找出存在的问题和解决方法。
15. _____ 我评价自己学习英语的策略，从而找出薄弱环节和改进的措施。
16. _____ 我根据学习的任务特点，选择不同的学习策略。
17. _____ 我选择适合自己水平的英语材料来学习。
18. _____ 我研究自己的个性特点，找出哪些特点有利于自己的英语学习，哪些特点阻碍自己的进步，从而能发挥自己的优势，采取相应的措施，克服弱点。
19. _____ 当成绩不理想时，我总是鼓励自己千万不能泄气。
20. _____ 有意识地训练自己的毅力。

方法策略：

21. _____ 为了提高自己的听力理解能力，课外我主动收听各种录音和英语广播。
22. _____ 当听英语材料时，我争取听懂每一句话的意思。
23. _____ 假如在听英语时遇到生词，我会跳过生词继续听下去。
24. _____ 假如在听英语材料时遇到生词，我会尽量记住生词的发音，然后根据发音在字典上查找它的拼写和意思。
25. _____ 在英语课上，我尽量争取回答问题。
26. _____ 我课外尽量地用英语与同学和老师（包括外教）会话。
27. _____ 我课外自己对自己说英语，练口语。
28. _____ 读课文时，我先通读全篇课文了解文章的概要，然后再理解每个句子的意思。
29. _____ 当阅读课文时我争取弄懂课文里的每一处。
30. _____ 在课文中碰到生词时，我结合上下文猜生词的意思。
31. _____ 我在课外主动阅读英文报纸、杂志或小说。
32. _____ 我主动用英语记笔记、留言、写信或日记。
33. _____ 当我查词典时，我会注意一个词的各种意思及所给的例句。
34. _____ 当在字典上查到某个生词时，我只找出与课文内容有关的意思。

35. _____ 我用重复多遍的方法来记生词。
36. _____ 记单词时,我会想到同根的词。
37. _____ 记单词时,我会联想有关的同义词或反义词。
38. _____ 学习新语法时,我会阅读语法书,了解语法的规则。
39. _____ 学习新语法时,我会做句型练习。
40. _____ 学习新语法内容时,我会把它们与中文进行对比。

4.2 A Thesis on Linguistics

On the Meanings of the Number SEVEN in the Eastern and Western Culture

Abstract

Numbers are invented to meet the needs of society by the help of symbols, signs and semiotics when human beings develop to a certain stage. Owing to the influence of the eastern and western tradition, religious belief, language worship, there are different apotheoses of the numbers between the east and west. However, there are many common features and similar laws, especially in the worship of numbers. Scholars at home and abroad have written many articles and works about numbers but few of them have explored the connotations of a specific number in eastern and western cultures from the perspective of semiotics. This thesis first of all summarizes the origin and developing stages of numerology, followed by the interpretation of connotations, denotations and the symbolic meanings about SEVEN from semiotics. Later, the article presents the applications of SEVEN in culture and daily life of the eastern and western society, attempting to further compare the connotations, denotations and the symbolic meanings of the number SEVEN in the east and west. With abundant examples, the paper aims at proving that the connotations and the symbolic meanings of numbers can reflect culture as well as a mode of thinking and behavior.

Key words: semiotics, the number SEVEN, culture, meaning

摘　　要

　　数字是人类思维发展到一定阶段,为适应社会生产活动的需要,在符号的帮助下产生的。由于受东西方文化传统、宗教信仰、语言崇拜、地理环境等方面的影响,数字的神化存在着东西方差异,但也存在着共性,有着共同的规律,特别体现在数字"七"上。国内有不少学者就数字写过著作和论文,但是极少有人从社会符号学的角度探讨一个具体的数字在东西方文化中的含义。本文先介绍了数字学的起源和发展,接着从社会符号学的角度解释了数字"七"的内涵、外延及象征意义。之后,文章分别列举了数字"七"在东西方社会、文化、生活上面的运用,从而进一步分析数字"七"在东西方所代表的文化内涵和象征意义,以及它们的相同点和不同点。文章旨在通过列举大量的例子证明数字的文化内涵和象征意义可以反映一种文化、一种思维及一种行为模式。

关键词:社会符号学,数字"七",文化,含义

Contents

Abstract ·· (Ⅰ)
摘要 ·· (Ⅱ)
1 Introduction ·· (1)
2 Numerology Review ··· (3)
   2.1 History of Numerology ·· (3)
   2.2 The Meanings of Meaning ··· (4)
   2.3 The Meanings of the Number SEVEN ··· (4)
      2.3.1 The Denotative Meanings of the Number SEVEN ························ (4)
      2.3.2 The Connotative Meanings of the Number SEVEN ······················ (5)
3 The Application of the Number SEVEN ·· (6)
   3.1 The Application of the Number SEVEN in the East ······························· (6)
      3.1.1 The Application of the Number SEVEN in Eastern Society ············ (6)
      3.1.2 The Application of the Number SEVEN in Eastern Literature ········· (7)
      3.1.3 The Application of the Number SEVEN in Eastern Daily Life ········· (8)
   3.2 The Application of the Number SEVEN in the West ······························ (9)
      3.2.1 The Application of the Number SEVEN in Western Society ··········· (9)
      3.2.2 The Application of the Number SEVEN in Western Literature ······· (10)
      3.2.3 The Application of the Number SEVEN in Western Daily Life ······· (12)
4 Conclusion ··· (16)
Bibliography ··· (17)

1 Introduction

Culture exists in the internal and external modes. It learns and disseminates itself by the help of signs and constructs the special attainments of the human beings (A. L. Robert and K. Clark, 1952). In China, culture is called "Wenhua". From the ancient Chinese books, "Wen" means the works, the characteristics, the laws and rites, "Hua" means enlightening people by education. From the aspect of politics, "Wenhua" is used to enlighten people to be governed by the emperors. In the West, culture is from the Latin word "cultura", referring to agriculture and growing. Since the fifteenth century, it has been used to mean fostering and developing the ability of human beings.

Culture includes the following matters: ① the mental factor, also called the spirit culture, refers to philosophy, science, art, religion, moral and concept of value—the core of the spirit culture, which is of the most significance; ② language and signs, they are the methods that culture accumulates and builds up. Human beings can only communicate through language and signs, and only communication and interaction can create culture (王福祥,1997,63).

Numbers are invented to meet the needs of society by the help of symbols, signs and semiotics when human beings develop to a certain stage (苏金智,1991, 23). Numerology is a special field in linguistics. In the scientific numerology world, the function of number is to compute, though, in another world—the mind of human beings, its function is to express and represent. Many numbers have become imaginary numbers or fate numbers. They have abundant denotative meanings as well as connotative meanings (王秉钦,1998, 66).

Due to the influence of the eastern and western tradition, religious belief, language worship, there are different apotheoses of the numbers between the East and West. Besides, there are many things in common and similar laws, especially in the worship of number. The easterners have their fate numbers, so do the westerners. The developing process of mysterious number always has three stages:apotheoses,generation,imagination (王秉钦,1998, 35).

Semiotics, as the study of how people use and understand signs, is as old as the writings of Plato and Aristotle, but its present-day formulations depend on the unusual insights of Ferdinand de Saussure and Charles Peirce. The linguistic sign is made of the union of a concept and a sound image. The meaning of any sign is found in the association created between the sound image and the concept. According to Saussure, language is a set of sign system (Saussure, 1966, 16). A more common way to define a linguistic sign is

· 1 ·

that a sign is the combination of a signifier and a signified. Saussure says the sound image is the signifier and the concept the signified (Saussure, 1966, 21). You can also think of a word as a signifier and the thing it represents as a signified (though technically these are called sign and referent, respectively). The sign, as union of a signifier and a signified, has two main characteristics. The bond between the signifier and signified is arbitrary (Fisk, 1982, 47).

Charles Peirce categorized three types of relations between sign and meaning: ① iconic — a sign that resembles its object, iconic signs are based on the similarities between the literal meaning of a sign and reference; ② indexical — a sign that is factually linked to its object, indexical signs are based upon association rather than upon similarity; ③ symbolic — the shape, color, or function of a sign that represents the object. The cultural structure (the way in which a given society organizes the world which it perceives, analyzes and transforms) is a semiotic structure and therefore a system of units in which each unit can stand for another (Halliday, 1980, 52).

One of de Saussure's general assumptions was that language could be taken as a model semiotic system and that its basic concepts could be applied to other spheres of social and cultural life (it places undue restrictions on the concept of the sign and related ideas) (Halliday, 1980, 47).

Morris said the meaning of signs includes three aspects: designative meaning, connotative meaning and pragmatic meaning (Eugene A. Nida, 1993).

In society, we are surrounded by signs of various descriptions. They are the essence of human interaction. What we need is a set of coherent systems of classification, so that we can impose order on this seemingly disorderly situation. The sign in turn is a triadic relation: ① initiates identification of the sign; ② object of the sign; ③ interpretant or the effect of the sign. This paper is to study the meanings of the number SEVEN as a sign in the western and eastern culture from its designative meaning, connotative meaning and symbolic meaning.

2 Numerology Review

2.1 History of Numerology

  The study of numerology has been developing for many years. With the continuous, great and brilliant contributions made by various scholars, it has three major schools and branches, that is, the Kabbalah, the Chaldean and the Pythagorean.

  Generally speaking, the three major schools have made different contributions to numerology. Although they have few conflicts about the concepts and points of view on numbers, they emphasize different parts when interpreting. Therefore, the scholars intersect these different theories for reference on different occasions.

  The Kabbalah, originated from the mysticism of Greece, believes that knowledge does accompany with the soul and minds of human beings, not the education systems that people have designed. It derives from the Greek alphabet. Therefore, this school has only twenty-two vibrate numbers between one and four hundred.

  The alphabet of the New Kabbalah is created according to Roman alphabet, not Greek. In addition to that, when discussing numerology, the New Kabbalah focuses on another part. They stress the developing process of the whole thing, not limited to the characteristics of human beings. The numerology regular of the New Kabbalah is the same as that of the Pythagorean. For instance, the method of calculating year is from the New Kabbalah.

  The Chaldean, whose arithmetic has its own system since ancient Babylon while adding some concepts of astrology, considers number nine as a pretty holy number because it is dependent from the other vibrate numbers, not corresponding with any other alphabets. This is a notable difference from the rest schools. The Chaldean always used the concept of complex number or plural number.

  The Pythagorean school is established by Pythagorean. When he was studying mathematics and arithmetic, Pythagorean was extremely interested in supernatural and mysterious doctrine. He had done some researches in an Egypt alchemy school and put what he achieved into the skills and methods of teaching to his Greek students. His students not only wrote these theories by hand but also learnt them by heart. In addition, Pythagorean had discovered "The Right Triangle", which was used to represent the individual as well as an interpretive text to the life of human beings.

2.2 The Meanings of Meaning

Meaning has always been a central topic in human scholarship, though the term "semantics" has only a history of a little over a hundred years. There were discussions of meaning in the works of the Greek philosopher Plato as early as in the fifth century before Christ. In China, Lao Zi had discussed similar questions even earlier. The fact that over the years numerous dictionaries have been produced with a view to explaining the meanings of words also witnesses its long tradition. The subject concerning the study of meaning is called semantics. More specifically, semantics is the study of the meaning of linguistic units, words and sentences in particular（胡壮麟，2001,158）.

One difficulty in the study of meaning is that the word "meaning" itself has different meanings. In their book ***The Meaning of Meaning*** written in 1923, C. K. Ogden and I. A. Richards present a "representative list of the main definitions which reputable students of meaning have favored"(p. 186). G. Leech in a more moderate tone recognizes seven types of meaning in his *Semantics* (p. 23), first published in 1974, as follows.

(1) Conceptual meaning: logical, cognitive, or denotative content.

(2) Connotative meaning: what is communicated by virtue of what language refers to.

(3) Social meaning: what is communicated of the social circumstances of language use.

(4) Affective meaning: what is communicated of the feelings and attitudes of the speaker/writer.

(5) Reflected meaning: what is communicated through association with another sense of the same expression.

(6) Collocative meaning: what is communicated through association with words which tend to occur in the environment of another word.

(7) Thematic meaning: what is communicated by the way in which the message is organized in terms of order and emphasis.

Leech says that the first type of meaning—conceptual meaning—makes up the central part. It is "denotative" in that it is concerned with the relationship between a word and the thing it denotes, or refers to. In this sense, conceptual meaning overlaps to a large extent with the notion of reference. But the term connotative used in the name of the second type of meaning is used in a sense different from that in philosophical discussions. Philosophers use connotation, opposite to denotation, to mean the properties of the entity a word denotes.

2.3 The Meanings of the Number SEVEN

2.3.1 The Denotative Meanings of the Number SEVEN

Semiotics takes the number SEVEN as a text to analyze, the objective of which is to study the meaning system produced from the text, and the special signs, symbols, and the structure of the text. Analyzing denotative meanings of the number SEVEN is to discover the common and external meanings, the regularity and the structure of the sign of the number SEVEN. This study adopts two kinds of methods.

(1) Diachronic analysis: refers to the structure relation of syntagm, considering the text as a continuous link of the thing to analyze the narrating structure (Fisk, 1982, 62; Berger, 1987, 14). The meaning of the number SEVEN is one more than six, having seven of the thing specified.

(2) Synchronic analysis: analyzes the paradigm of the sign. From a group of related factors, choose the factors or units which are needed. All the units in the same group must have the same characteristics, but each unit could distinguish from the rest in this group as well (Fisk, 1986, 61). Synchronic analysis of the text is to find the invisible opposite mode and the meaning produced (Berger, 1987, 145).

This paper studies the synchronic analysis of the number SEVEN, aiming to compare the various opinions and views on it between the East and West, and their similarities and differences in the texts.

2.3.2 The Connotative Meanings of the Number SEVEN

This paper studies the social and cultural meanings of the number SEVEN except the denotative meaning and presenting structure. The connotative meaning includes two parts. One refers to the social and cultural value, which is always a myth. The relation between a signifier and a signified is arbitrary, although the sign could represent the nature and the essence. But the text links to certain social and cultural meanings, and therefore the sign is the process of choice and combination, representing the catalog and the distinction of the reality (Barthes, 1972, 113). Through the analysis of the social myth, we can interpret the connotative meanings of the number SEVEN, and it reflects the social and cultural value system while influencing the social value and the knowledge system. Affected by the value, life experience, emotions, culture, and religion of the signer, the number SEVEN means samsara, destiny, reincarnation, the ending and a brand new beginning, satisfaction after a lot of suffering in the East (Barthes, 1968, 89, 1972, 115; Seiter, 1987, 29-30). While the number SEVEN refers to the magic and holy power of the God, mystery, completeness and perfection, samsara, the ending and a brand new beginning, satisfaction after a lot of suffering, occult, happiness and luck in the West. The similarity is that the connotative meanings of the number SEVEN in the East and West both have the meaning of "samsara, the ending and a brand new beginning, satisfaction after a lot of suffering". The number SEVEN has such abundant meanings that people both in the east and west like it and apply it to every aspect of life.

3 The Application of the Number SEVEN

3.1 The Application of the Number SEVEN in the East

3.1.1 The Application of the Number SEVEN in Eastern Society

In the East, on the basis of *Analytical Dictionary of Chinese Characters* (《说文解字》) and *Nine Chapters on the Mathematical Art* (《九章算术》), the number SEVEN only means a number, which is one more than six. However, the symbolic meaning of the number SEVEN is influenced by Confucianism, Buddhism and Taoism to a larger extent. It stresses on destiny, samsara, reincarnation, transmigration, the ending and a brand new beginning after a lot of suffering.

For example, there is an interesting fable from *Book of Master Zhuang/Chuang Tzu* (《庄子》). The Emperor of the South Sea is known as Shu (Change). The Emperor of the North Sea is called Hu (Dramatic). The Emperor of the Center is called Hun-tun (Chaos). Shu and Hu met every so often in the region of Hun-tun. Hun-tun always treated them kindly and virtuously. Shu and Hu said, "Everyone has seven orifices so they can see, hear, eat and breathe. Hun-tun does not have these. Let us bore some holes into him." Each day they bored a hole into Hun-tun, but on the seventh day Hun-tun died.

With this fable, Zhuang Zi aims to make it clear that man should not be allowed to tamper at will with what is created by nature. This is the so-called Lao-Zhuang philosophy of "govern by doing nothing that goes against nature"(无为而治). It has little in common with philosophy of Buddhism, according to which everything has its destiny and benevolence merit. Things form cause and start from pratitya-samutpada (万事皆缘起); however, sunya is rupa (in Buddhism it means everything visible is empty).

In *Analects of Confucius* (《论语》), Confucius says, "At fifteen, I set my heart upon learning. At thirty, I had planted my feet firm upon the ground. At forty, I no longer suffered from perplexities. At fifty, I knew what were the biddings of heaven. At sixty, I heard them with docile ear. At seventy, I could follow the dictates of my own heart, for what I desired no longer overstepped the boundaries of right." (子曰:"吾十有五而志于学,三十而立,四十而不惑,五十而知天命,六十而耳顺,七十而从心所欲,不逾矩。")Because after the seventh of ten years, which seems a reincarnation, people have meditative minds and realize the truth. So he says "I could follow the dictates of my own heart, for what I desired no longer overstepped the boundaries of right". The outside laws are transformed into the internal ethics and morality.

From those above, we can see that the sign SEVEN is a reflection of traditional culture and religious belief. The connotative meaning of the number SEVEN is destiny and samsara influenced by Confucianism, Buddhism and Taoism. But when people use the number SEVEN to interpret a thing or enlighten people, it affects the main philosophy of the society in an invisible way.

3.1.2 The Application of the Number SEVEN in Eastern Literature

Intrigues of the Warring States records that Yao, one of the "Five Great Emperors" in the ancient times, has nine advisers and Shun, the earliest ancestor of Shang Dynasty, has seven helpful friends (《战国策》:尧有九佐,舜有七友。). In *Records of the Grand Historian*, Bao Shenxu — the censor-in-chief of Chu State, cried for the whole seven days and nights in the front of the Qin palace, asking for the army to save his country. Finally, the Emperor of Qin was moved by his loyalty, and sent troops to help his country.(《史记》——包申胥立于秦廷,昼夜哭,七日七夜不绝其声。秦哀公怜之,曰:"楚虽无道,有臣若是,可无存乎!"乃遣车五百乘救楚击吴。) *Romance of the Three Kingdoms*(《三国演义》) says that Zhu Geliang, the famous chief of counselor in Shu Kingdom, captured and freed Meng Huo for seven times. At last, Meng Huo was touched by this virtue, came over and pledged allegiance to Zhu Geliang. Cao Zhi, the son of Cao Cao, the Emperor of Wei Dynasty during the three kingdoms period, wrote the famous poem in seven steps.

In these great and compelling stories, the number SEVEN is a symbol that only if you suffer a lot but still have a strong will can you get what you want. Its connotation is satisfaction after a lot of suffering, the ending and a brand new beginning.

Bai Juyi, the brilliant and famous poet from the ordinary people in Tang Dynasty, wrote the great poem *A Song of Unending Sorrow*(《长恨歌》)—"On the seventh day of the seventh-month, in the Palace of Long Life, we told each other secretly in the quiet midnight world that we wished to fly in heaven, two birds with the wings of one, and to grow together on the earth, two branches of one tree. Earth endures, heaven endures; some time both shall end, while this unending sorrow goes on and on forever". Meng Jiangnv, an ordinary female, whose husband was captured to build the Great Wall but disappeared, cried for seven days and nights. The cry was so sorrowful that the Great Wall was collapsed and her husband appeared.

The philosophy of Bai Juyi combines the philosophy of Buddhism, Taoism and Confucianism. He categorizes his poems into three types and considers that the satiric poems represent his willingness to save and harmonize the world, while the leisurely and comfortable poems state his wish to be left alone. *A Song of Unending Sorrow* on one hand satirizes that the destruction is caused by the Emperor himself; on the other hand, denotes a kind of destiny and reincarnation, so does the story of Meng Jiangnv.

Zhang Xianzhong, an extremely evil man in the late Ming Dynasty who slaughtered a great number of old men, women and children, made the "Seven Kills the Tablet"(张献中《七杀碑》).

In the long and brilliant eastern literary history, the great people, such as Yao, Shun, or the ordinary people, like Meng Jiangnv, or the evil man, all prefer the number SEVEN. The connotative meaning of it is satisfaction after a lot of suffering, the ending and a brand new beginning, destiny and reincarnation affected by Buddhism, Taoism and Confucianism. The scholars and writers apply the sign to the literature to disseminate the main philosophy of the society. The great literature and stories are left and kept. The descendants learn and are influenced. The number SEVEN, as a sign, reflects the main philosophy of the society at different times.

3.1.3 The Application of the Number SEVEN in Eastern Daily Life

In ancient times of Chinese society, husbands can forsake their wives for seven reasons according to the **Da Dai Liji**(《大戴礼记》), which is called seven quits or seven abandons. A husband can abandon his wife rightly if she is not filial, has no son, is wanton, tends to be jealous, has serious disease, is gossipy or steals. **Compendium of Materia Medica**(《本草纲目》) records that the female has menses during the second of seven years, which means fourteen years old, and finishes it after the seventh of seven years, referring to forty-nine years old. To be a musician in the Chinese feudal society, one must master seven tunes, which are Gong, Shang, Jue, BianZhi, Zhi, Yu, BianGong.

These signs of SEVEN are fixed by the law of the traditional culture. However, with the development of the society, some signs of SEVEN are never used any more in practice, but instead it was only kept as a mode of culture.

Human beings not only have six senses (eye, ear, nose, tongue, body and mind) but also own seven apertures. Besides, people have seven emotions, that is joy, wrath, sorrow, happiness, love, hate and lust. The seven common things in daily life are firewood, rice, oil, salt, thick sauce, vinegar and tea. To be more elegant, we should enjoy another seven talents and skills, which are Chinese zither, chess, calligraphy, painting, poem, wine and flower arranging. Because the number SEVEN has the symbolic meanings, the social value makes the things related to SEVEN special, considering it as a kind of destiny, a mode of deeds.

Influenced by the life experience, when mentioning the lovers, we will remember Niu Lang and the goddess Zhi Nv on 7th, July in lunar calendar. Also in the ancient astrology, there are twenty-eight constellations called the lunar mansions. From the aspects of east, west, south and north, each direction has seven constellations. The Big Dipper has seven stars, too. In **Almanac**(《历书》), the seventh month of the lunar calendar is called "Gua

Month". In Heavenly Stems, Geng is the seventh of the ten "Heavenly Stems". In "Earthly Branches", Wu is the seventh of the 12 "Earthly Branches". In wind scale, force seven wind is called moderate gale as well. As we all know, the rainbow has seven colors, which are, red, orange, yellow, green, azure (dark green), blue and purple. It is based on the seven colors of the rainbow that people invent the seven-piece puzzle or the magic square. In optics, the white light can be proved by the seven-light instrument that the white light is the combination of the seven lights.

The connotations of the sign are affected by the culture, religion, the social value and life experience. People learn the sign SEVEN from the literature and apply it to the social activities in daily life. With the generalization of the sign SEVEN, more and more things are related to it. People prefer it and integrate the number SEVEN into the new culture.

3.2　The Application of the Number SEVEN in the West

3.2.1　The Application of the Number SEVEN in Western Society

In western society, the number SEVEN is a both holy and secret number. With the rising and the development of religion, the number SEVEN is given rich symbolic meanings and permeates in every aspect of the society. The western rulers and religion always adopt the number SEVEN to regularize the behavior and soul of human beings. The following are some examples.

The Seven Heavens(七重天)：the first heaven is pure silver（纯银天）, the living place for Adam and Eve; the second is pure gold（纯金天）, the manor of John and Jesus; the third is pearl（珍珠天）; the fourth is white gold（白金天）, where the wine and tear angels live in; the fifth is silver（银天）, where the revenge angel resides; the sixth is ruby and garnet（红宝石天）, where the guard angel lives in; the seventh is the extreme happy（极乐天）, the living place for the God and the superior angel. The English idiom "to be in the seventh heaven" means extremely happy.

The Seven Champions（基督教的七大守护神）：ST. George of England（英格兰的圣·乔治）, ST. Andrew of Scotland（苏格兰的圣·安德鲁）, ST. Patrick of Ireland（爱尔兰的圣·帕特里奇）, ST. David of Wales（威尔士的圣·大卫）, ST. Denis of France（法兰西的圣·丹尼斯）, ST. James of Spain（西班牙的圣·詹姆斯）, ST. Anthony of Italy（意大利的圣·安东尼）.

The above are the basic knowledge of Christianity. The following are the suggestions given by God, hoping human beings can purify their souls and discipline themselves from the aspect of mind.

The Seven Gifts of the Spirit（神的七大礼物）：wisdom（智慧）, understanding（理解）, counsel（忠告）, fortitude（毅力）, knowledge（知识）, piety（虔诚）, fear of the Lord（畏上帝）.

The Seven Virtues (七大美德)：faith (信任), hope (希望), charity (仁慈), justice (公正), fortitude (毅力), prudence (谨慎), temperance (节制).

The Seven Deadly Sins (七宗罪)：pride (骄傲), wrath (发怒), envy (嫉妒), lust (肉欲), gluttony (贪吃), avarice (贪婪), sloth (懒惰).

Besides the good qualities that God hopes people can possess, he also illustrates the behaviors to guide and restrict people.

The Seven Sacraments (七大圣事)：baptism (圣洗), confirmation (坚振), eucharist (圣餐礼), penance (告解), ordination (受圣职礼), matrimony (婚配), extreme unction (僧侣为垂死者行涂油礼).

The Seven Spiritual Works of Mercy (七大精神善事)：to convert the sinner (改造罪人), to instruct the ignorant (教育无知者), to counsel those in doubt (劝解疑惑者), to comfort those in sorrow (安慰痛苦的人), to bear wrongs patiently (耐心忍屈), to forgive the injuries (原谅伤者), to pray for the living and the dead (为生者和死者祈祷).

The Seven Corporal Works of Mercy (七大肉体善事)：to attend the sick (照顾病人), to feed the hungry (施食于饥者), to give the drink to the thirsty (施饮于渴者), to clothe the naked (施衣于裸者), to harbor the stranger (给陌生人住宿), to minister to prisoners (开导凶犯), to bury the dead (埋葬死者).

De Saussure once said that language would be taken as a model semiotic system and its basic concepts would be applied to other spheres of social and cultural life. Therefore, the number SEVEN represents the magic and holy power of God, as a sign in religion, gives the restrictions on people's deeds and minds.

3.2.2　The Application of the Number SEVEN in Western Literature

The number SEVEN is one of the most significant numbers in the *Holy Bible*. God takes the perfect world number "four" and added to it the perfect divine number "three", then gets SEVEN, the most sacred number to the Hebrews. It is earth crowned with heaven—the four-square earth plus the divine completeness of God. So we have SEVEN expressing completeness through union of earth with heaven. This number is used more than all other numbers in the words of God, save the number one.

The Scriptures say that there are seven Spirits of God (Rev. 3:1, 4:5, and 5:6). There are numerous places throughout the Scriptures where God denotes things in "sevens" or multiples of seven. SEVEN, as a text, is throughout the Scriptures. The following are some examples.

"Behold, there come **seven** *years of great plenty throughout all the land of Egypt*:" (***Genesis*** 41:29)

"*And there shall arise after them* **seven** *years of famine; and all the plenty shall be forgotten in the land of Egypt; and the famine shall consume the land* ;" (***Genesis*** 41:30)

"*And thou shalt the number* **seven** *sabbaths of years unto thee,* **seven** *times* **seven**

· 10 ·

years; and the space of the **seven** sabbaths of years shall be unto thee forty and nine years."(**Leviticus** 25∶8)

"And they that dwell in the cities of Israel shall go forth, and shall set on fire and burn the weapons, both the shields and the bucklers, the bows and the arrows, and the handstaves, and the spears, and they shall burn them with fire **seven** years:"(**Ezekiel** 39∶9)

"**Seventy** weeks are determined upon thy people and upon thy holy city, to finish the transgression, and to make an end of sins, and to make reconciliation for iniquity, and to bring in everlasting righteousness, and to seal up the vision and prophecy, and to anoint the most Holy."(**Daniel** 9∶24)

"And on the **seventh** day God ended his work which he had made; and he rested on the **seventh** day from all his work which he had made. And God blessed the **seventh** day, and sanctified it: because that in it he had rested from all his work which God created and made."(**Genesis** 2∶2-3)

The word "create" is used SEVEN times in connection with God's creative work. (**Genesis** 1∶1; **Genesis** 1∶21; 1∶27 (three times); 2∶3; and 2∶4). God appointed SEVEN days for the week. Jesus said to "forgive seventy times SEVEN". In other words, He is saying, "Keep on forgiving until you are complete." Even the duration of Israel's great punishments was based upon this law of SEVENS. Their captivity in Babylon was for seventy years, ten periods of SEVENS. Noah took the clean beasts into the ark by SEVENS (**Genesis** 7∶2). SEVEN days after Noah went into the ark the flood came (**Genesis** 7∶10). Those SEVEN days completed God's time of waiting.

"For in six days the LORD made heaven and earth, the sea, and all that in them is, and rested the **seventh** day: wherefore the LORD blessed the sabbath day, and hallowed it."(**Exodus** 20∶11)

"Six days shall work be done, but on the **seventh** day there shall be to you a holy day, a sabbath of rest to the LORD: whosoever doeth work therein shall be put to death." (**Exodus** 35∶2)

The number SEVEN and the Sabbath, which is the seventh day, are connected with the word "complete". The word "complete" follows the words "the seventh sabbath" (the seventh day). Following the seventh sabbath, there is something new that would take place. The whole word of God is founded upon the number SEVEN. It stands for the SEVENTH day of the Creation Week, and speaks of the Millennial Rest day. It denotes completeness or perfection.

And in **Revelation**, **New Testament**(《启示录》), there are also many things related with the number SEVEN.

"John to the **seven** churches which are in Asia: Grace be unto you, and peace, from him which is, and which was, and which is to come... I saw **seven** golden candlesticks... And he had in his right hand **seven** stars: and out of his mouth went a

· 11 ·

*sharp twoedged sword; and his countenance was as the sun shineth in his strength.... The mystery of the **seven** stars which thou sawest in my right hand, and the **seven** golden candlesticks. The **seven** stars are the angels of the **seven** churches; and the **seven** candlesticks which thou sawest are the **seven** churches. Unto the angel of the church of Ephesus write; These things saith he that holdeth the **seven** stars in his right hand, who walketh in the midst of the **seven** golden candlesticks... And unto the angel of the church in Sardis write; These things saith he that hath the **seven** Spirits of God, and the **seven** stars; I know thy works, that thou hast a name that thou livest, and art dead.... And out of the throne proceeded lightnings and thunderings and voices; And there were **seven** lamps of fire burning before the throne, which are the **seven** Spirits of God.... And I beheld, and, lo, in the midst of the throne and of the four beasts, and in the midst of the elders, stood a Lamb as it had been slain, having **seven** horns and **seven** eyes, which are the **seven** Spirits of God sent forth into all the earth.... But in the days of the voice of the **seventh** angel, when he shall begin to sound, the mystery of God should be finished... And the **seventh** angel poured out his vial into the air; And there came a great voice out of the temple of heaven, from the throne, saying, It is done."*

From these examples, we can see that the symbolic meaning of the number SEVEN in the west is the mysterious and holy power of God. In the Book of **Revelation** the number SEVEN is used throughout. There are SEVEN churches, SEVEN Spirits, SEVEN stars, SEVEN seals, SEVEN trumpets, SEVEN vials, SEVEN personages, SEVEN dooms, and SEVEN new things. SEVEN symbolizes spiritual perfection. All of life revolves around this number. SEVEN is used over 700 times in the **Bible**. It is used 54 times in the Book of **Revelation**. It is complete, occult, and absolute due to the mysterious and holy power of God. Just because of this, the number SEVEN becomes the fate number, as a symbol in the west. The word "finished" is connected with the number SEVEN. "It is done." (**Revelation** 16:17) is another expression found in connection with the number SEVEN in **Revelation**. So when the number SEVEN resembles a disaster or a calamity, it could never be avoided. But, following that glorious "the Seventh Day", the day which after will be a new first day, a new eternal beginning without end.

3.2.3 The Application of the Number SEVEN in Western Daily Life

Human physiology is constructed on a law of SEVENS. Children are born to mothers in a certain number of weeks, usually 280 days, which is a multiple of SEVENS. Fevers and intermittent attacks of gout, ague, and similar complaints have a period of operation of SEVEN, FOURTEEN or TWENTY-ONE days are known as critical days. Life operates in a cycle of SEVENS. Changes take place in the body every SEVEN years. There are SEVEN bones in the neck, and SEVEN holes in the head. Most births are multiple of SEVENS. It takes three weeks (21 days) to hatch hen's eggs; the pigeon needs two weeks (14 days), after having laid eggs.

The number SEVEN has a positive meaning in western society. When people throw something for competition, they consider the number SEVEN as a success. A lot of companies use it in their brand names, such as Mild Seven, Seven-eleven. For many places of interest and great, ancient people use SEVEN as their titles, such as: Seven Hills of Rome, the Seventh Avenue—the costume center in New York, Seven Sages in ancient Greece(Solon, Thales, Pittacus, Bias, Chilon, Cleobulus, Periander). People apply the connotative meaning "luck and happiness" of the number SEVEN, hoping the mysterious God can bring fortune and protect them.

Also, some films prefer the number SEVEN, such as *The Seven Year Itch*, *The Seven Deadly Sins*. No doubt, the latter links to religion. The name, as a symbol soon arouses the interest of the audience, and the connotation of this symbol makes this film profound and let people rethink.

The number SEVEN also appears in physics and chemistry. An example that almost everyone can relate to is Music. All the songs you hear on the radio are based on a musical system of just seven major notes(see Fig. 4-1).

Fig. 4-1

Notice that the seven notes repeat, with the eighth key a higher or lower octave of the first as you go up or down the keyboard. All other minor notes, sharps and flats, fit within the structure of the basic seven. The number SEVEN is applied to the inventions, but why it repeats only after seven notes make the number SEVEN more mysterious.

If you pass sunlight through a prism, it produces seven colors—three primary colors and four secondary ones(see Fig. 4-2).

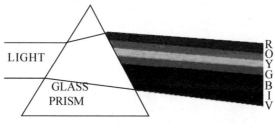

Fig. 4-2

In the realm of minerals and geochemistry, there are seven crystal systems(see Fig. 4-3).

Here is a picture of example minerals from each of the seven systems(see Fig. 4-4).

Even the Periodic Table of the known elements appears to have seven levels of periodicity(see Fig. 4-5).

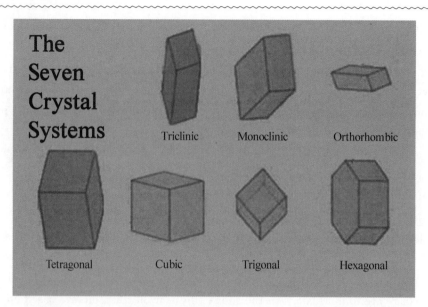

Fig. 4-3

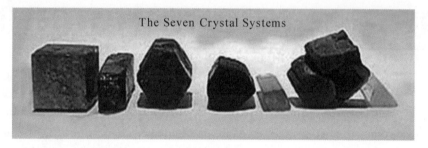

Fig. 4-4

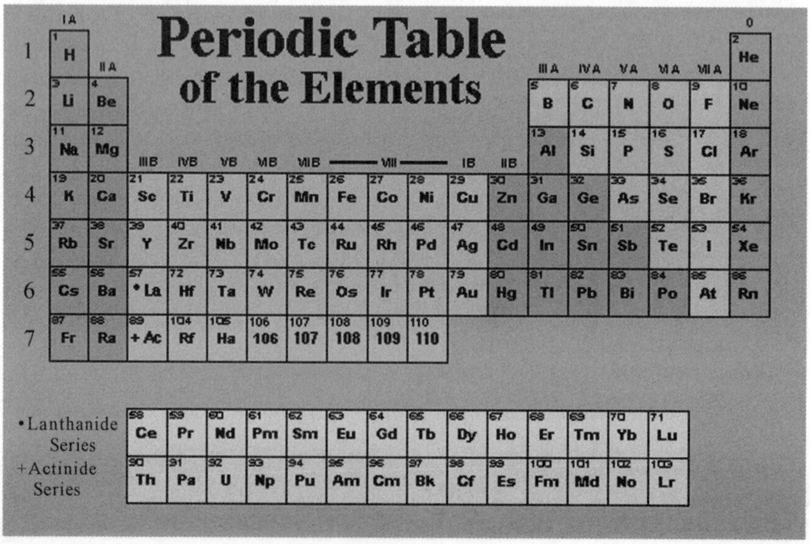

Fig. 4-5

In the west, people think that God has ordained a pattern of sevens in nature. All things of nature, be they matter, energy, time and space are designed and ordained by the Lord God. The SEVENS of God can be observed in the things of nature, and even physics and chemistry are structured on such a basic system.

4 Conclusion

It has long been acknowledged that language is an essential and important part of a given culture and that the impact of culture upon a given language is something intrinsic and indispensable. Though the endeavor in the pursuit of this inter-relationship has never been dominant in the development of linguistic science, "this very embedding of language in society and culture has been the focus of intense and sustained research efforts since the 1960s" (Apte 1994: 2000).

From the analyses above, we can make the conclusion that the culture affects and gives the connotative meanings of the sign, and people like to use the sign to interpret things because the speciality of the sign makes things more impressive and profound. When more and more people learn and understand it, the connotations of the sign are fixed and generalized in daily life. The culture creates the sign, and the sign interprets the culture. In another word, they mutually influence and interact. To sum up, the sign reflects a culture, a mode of mind and deed.

The number SEVEN is a reflection. The denotative meaning of the number SEVEN means the number, one more than six. Owing to the influence of the eastern and western tradition, religious belief and language worship, there are different apotheoses of the numbers between the East and the West. The similarity is that both of them have the connotative meaning "samsara, the ending and a brand new beginning, satisfaction after a lot of suffering". However, in the East, in Chinese feudal society, people's beliefs are affected by Confucianism, Buddhism and Taoism. They apply the sign to literature, disseminating the main philosophy of the society. The descendants learn and accept them. Later, it frequently appears in the social activities and integrates into the new culture, enlightening people and influencing the social value and the knowledge system. Therefore, the symbolic meanings of the number SEVEN are influenced by Confucianism, Buddhism and Taoism to a larger extent. It stresses on destiny, reincarnation and samsara—the ending and a brand new beginning, satisfaction after a lot of suffering. In the meantime, affected by the western religious belief, the connotative meanings of the number SEVEN refer to the magic and holy power of the God, mystery, completeness and perfection, happiness and luck, destiny in western society.

Bibliography

[1] BAR-TAL D, KRUGLANSKI A. The social psychology of knowledge [M]. London: Cambridge University Press, 1988.

[2] BLOCH B, TRAGER G. Outline of linguistic analysis [M]. Baltimore: Linguistic Society of America, 1987.

[3] NIDA E. Language, culture, and translating [M]. Shanghai: Shanghai Foreign Language Education Press, 1993.

[4] FISHMAN J A. Sociolinguistics [M]. New York: Newbury House Publishers, 1977.

[5] HALLIDAY M A K. Language as social semiotic [M]. Pittsburgh: University of Pittsburgh Press, 1980.

[6] LYONS J. Linguistic semantic: an introduction [M]. London: Cambridge University Press, 1995.

[7] The study of gemology [DB/OL]. http://yourgemologist.com.

[8] 戴炜栋, 何兆熊. 新编简明英语语言学教程 [M]. 上海: 上海外语教育出版社, 2004.

[9] 何善芬. 英汉语言对比研究 [M]. 上海: 上海外语教育出版社, 2002.

[10] 胡壮麟. 语言学教程 [M]. 北京: 北京大学出版社, 2002.

[11] 马克斯·韦伯. 儒教与道教 [M]. 南京: 江苏人民出版社, 1997.

[12] 王秉钦. 语言与翻译新论 [M]. 天津: 南开大学出版社, 1998.

[13] 王福祥. 文化与语言（论文集）[M]. 上海: 外语教学与研究出版社, 1997.

[14] 苏金智. 数的灵物崇拜 [J]. 语言、社会、文化, 1991(1).

[15] 汤一介. 中国传统文化中的儒释道 [M]. 北京: 中国和平出版社, 1988.

[16] 中国社科院世界宗教研究所佛教研究室. 佛教文化面面观 [M]. 济南: 齐鲁书社, 2000.

[17] 中国社科院世界宗教研究所基督教研究室. 基督教文化面面观 [M]. 济南: 齐鲁书社, 2000.

4.3 A Thesis on Translation

Translation Error Analysis of English Majors

Abstract

In order to help students with their translation and assist teachers to find out main problems of students in their translation, this article studies an English to Chinese translation exercise of the second year English majors of the school of foreign languages in Wuhan Institute of Technology. It first collects and sorts out the typical errors made by students and then analyzes the causes of the errors guided by error analysis theory. The research adopts the basic translation criteria of TEM-8 in dealing with students' translations. According to the research, students have made quite a few errors, mainly in choosing denotation or connotation of words, producing idiomatic Chinese expressions, translating proper nouns and misinterpretation of sentences. This thesis attempts to find out the reasons why they made all these errors and put forward some suggestions for improving the quality of translation teaching and enabling students to enjoy the process of translation.

Key words: translation, error analysis, translation teaching, suggestions

摘　　要

　　为了使学生认识到自己翻译水平的不足,同时帮助教师发现学生在翻译过程中出现的主要问题,进而达到提高英语本科翻译课程的教学质量的目的。本文以武汉工程大学外语学院英语专业二年级学生为研究对象,采用以错误分析理论为基础,以基本翻译原则和英语专业八级翻译要求为指导的方法,对学生的一次英译汉翻译练习进行分析,收集学生练习中典型的翻译错误并分析错误产生的原因。研究中发现学生的翻译中存在许多错误,主要表现在词的本义和引申义选择、措辞不符合汉语表达习惯、专有名词翻译以及对复杂句的理解等四个方面。通过分析错误产生的原因,本文不仅试图帮助学生从错误中汲取教训,同时也为翻译教学方法提供一些改进建议,让学生们不再害怕翻译,而是学会享受翻译的过程,最终提高翻译水平。

关键词:翻译,错误分析,翻译教学,建议

Contents

Abstract ·· (Ⅰ)

摘要 ·· (Ⅱ)

1　Introduction ·· (1)

2　Theoretical Preliminaries ··· (2)

　2.1　Background Theory: Error Analysis Theory ··· (2)

　2.2　Translation Criteria ·· (3)

　　2.2.1　Translation Criteria at Home and Abroad ·· (3)

　　2.2.2　Basic Translation Criteria of TEM-8 for English Majors ················· (3)

3　Experiment ·· (5)

　3.1　Description of the Study ··· (5)

　　3.1.1　Purpose of the Study ··· (5)

　　3.1.2　Subjects ·· (5)

　　3.1.3　Materials ·· (6)

　3.2　Findings and Analysis ·· (6)

　　3.2.1　Findings ·· (6)

　　3.2.2　Error Analysis ·· (8)

　　3.2.3　Implications ··· (11)

4　Suggestions for Translation Teaching ·· (12)

　4.1　Enhancing Translation Responsibility ·· (12)

　4.2　Improving Context Awareness ··· (12)

　4.3　More Training in Translation Skills and More Instruction ····················· (13)

　4.4　Improving Chinese Competence ·· (13)

5　Conclusion ··· (14)

Bibliography ·· (15)

Appendix:英译汉参考译文 ··· (17)

1 Introduction

A new and dynamic era for translation has emerged since China adopted its "reform and opening up" policy. Moreover, China has embraced world since WTO entry. The exchange between China and other countries has been keeping increasing and expanding, covering such diverse fields as economics, commerce, science and technology, etc. Along with the economic boom, qualified translators and interpreters are needed in increasing numbers by all sorts of institutions. As a result, the education of translators faces a great challenge in terms of both quality and quantity.

On the other hand, the studies on translation errors of college English majors are few, especially on the basis of error analysis, which can be shown by the results searched by the author of these on China Academic Journal Electronic Publishing House on line. With translation error analysis as key words, only 11 articles can be found. The relevant articles are on *Translation Problems of juniors among English Majors* and *How Juniors among English Majors Improve E-C translation Competence* written by Yang Shizhuo. Only one master's thesis named *On Translation Teaching of Undergraduates—an Error Analysis of C-E Translation* is a study on students' translation errors based on statistics. Actually, translation teachers are often confronted with large numbers of errors in the students' translations, especially at the beginning. Through analysis of these errors, teachers, researchers and students can find out the reasons of these errors. Error analysis theory, though developed from second language teaching and research, can also be used in translation teaching and research in which the process involves the command of two languages.

Translation is a complex process, especially for the beginners. This thesis deals with the topic of translation error analysis in seven parts. First of all, it provides error analysis theory and the translation criteria for our error analysis. Later, on the basis of translation criteria of TEM-8 for English majors, this paper studies an exercise of the second year English majors through sorting out the error types, and analyzes the causes of the errors. Through this error analysis, we find out that students' errors mainly consist of choosing denotation or connotation of words, producing idiomatic Chinese expressions, translating proper nouns and misinterpretation of sentences. This thesis attempts to find out the reasons why students made all these errors, and then put forward some useful suggestions to improve translation teaching.

2 Theoretical Preliminaries

2.1 Background Theory: Error Analysis Theory

　　Human learning is fundamentally a process that involves making mistakes. Mistakes, misjudgments, miscalculations, and erroneous assumptions virtually form an important aspect of learning any skill. Second language learning is a process that is clearly unlike the first language learning in its trial-and-error nature. Inevitably, learners will make mistakes in the process of acquisition, and will even impede that process if they do not commit errors, and then benefit from various forms of feedbacks on those errors in turn.

　　Learners do make errors and these errors can be observed, analyzed, and classified to reveal something in common of the system operating within the learner. This fact leads to a surge of study of learners' errors, called error analysis. Here "error" generally refers to the learner's misuse or misunderstanding of the target language, whether it is grammatical or pragmatic. Error analysis is distinguished from contrastive analysis by its examination of errors attributable to all possible sources, not just those which result from negative transfer of the native language.

　　As Corder (1981) noted, "A learner's errors ... are significant in that they provide to the researcher evidence of how language is learned or acquired, what strategies or procedures the learner is employing in the discovery of the language." Errors are significant in three different ways: ① they tell the teacher, if he undertakes a systematic analysis, how far towards the goal the learner has progressed and consequently what remains for the learner to learn; ② they provide the researcher with evidence of how language is learned or acquired, what strategies or procedures the learner is employing in his discovery of the language; ③ they are indispensable to the learner himself, because we can regard the making of errors as a device which the learner uses in order to learn. It is a way the learner uses to test his hypothesis about the nature of the language that he is learning. The making of errors then is a strategy employed both by children acquiring their mother tongue and adults learning a second language.

　　Error analysis needs to collect and identify the errors made by the second language learners in order to classify and explain them. It is usually carried out in three procedures: recognizing errors, describing the error types and explaining the reasons. Errors are no longer seen as undesirability, but as a guide to the inner workings of the language learning process.

· 2 ·

Though error analysis is developed from second language teaching and research, it is very enlightening in translation teaching and research, in which the process also involves the use of two languages. Translation teachers are often confronted with large numbers of errors in the students' translations, especially at the beginning. Based on error analysis theory, this paper adopts the attitude that errors are not undesirable and can serve as a guide to the inner workings of translation process. In the analysis part, students' errors in translation will be analyzed in the similar procedures: recognizing errors, describing error types and explaining the reasons. This study attempts to find out what errors the students are most likely to make and causes for their errors as well, so as to find out what hinders students from properly reproducing the original message in another language.

2.2 Translation Criteria

2.2.1 Translation Criteria at Home and Abroad

In the history of translation research and practice, there have been translation criteria of different descriptions. For example, Yan Fu's three-character criteria "faithfulness, expressiveness, and elegance"; Lu Xun's "faithfulness is in preference to smoothness" (Liu Jingzhi, 1981: 13); Lin Yutang's "faithfulness, smoothness and beauty"; Fu Lei held "spiritual resemblance", that is, "what is more important is not the resemblance in form, but the resemblance in spirit"(1999: 68); Qian Zhongshu set forth his "hua"(1985: 302); Prof. Liu Zhongde adapted Yan Fu's three-criteria into "faithfulness—to be faithful to the content of the original, expressiveness—to be as expressive as the original, closeness—to be as close to the original style as possible"(1990: 24); Alexander Fraser Tytler laid down three general rules for a good translation: the translation should give a complete transcript of the ideas of the original work, the style and manner of writing should be of the same character with that of the original, the translation should have all the ease of the original composition(Shen Yuping, 2002: 167); and Eugene A. Nada's "functional equivalence" (1993: 116); Peter Newmark's "semantic translation" and "communicative translation" (2001: 39), etc.

2.2.2 Basic Translation Criteria of TEM-8 for English Majors

The general translation criteria mentioned in the above paragraphs may be too high for students, as translation beginners, to accomplish. Let's look at some specific translation criteria put forth in the Test Syllabus of TEM-8. TEM-8 is used to inspect whether the seniors majoring in English meet the requirements of band 8 prescribed by the National Teaching Syllabus for English Majors of Institutions of Higher Learning (2000), which states the aims of translation teaching as the immediate aims and ultimate aim. The immediate aims are to train students to translate texts of various types, to compare English and Chinese from various perspectives with the help of the basic translation theory, and to train students to use the fundamental translation techniques. The ultimate aim is to equip students with translation skills to deal satisfactorily with the translation tasks they are likely to be required to fulfill in real life.

The present Test Syllabus of TEM-8 (2004) has put forward the specific demand of the test form and time limits of the translation part: "the translation should be faithful to the source text with smooth expression and appropriate choice of words". The translation part is divided into two sections. One is to translate a passage on a journal in China or some Chinese literary works to English at the speed of 250~300 Chinese characters per hour. The translation should reproduce the entire original message with only 1 or 2 minor errors in vocabulary, syntax, spelling or punctuation. It should appropriately choose words and sentences with a wide variety. The other section is to translate a passage on a British or American journal or some English literary works into Chinese at the speed of 250~300 words per hour. The translation should faithfully reproduce the entire original message with only 1 or 2 minor lexical errors in Chinese. It should adequately reflect the style and tone of the original passage. The translation should be smooth with appropriate choice of words and sentence patterns.

3 Experiment

3.1 Description of the Study

3.1.1 Purpose of the Study

Error analysis has yielded insights into the second language acquisition process and has stimulated major changes in teaching practice. Likewise translation error analysis might yield insights into translation process which will help both the translators and the translation teachers.

Through this error recognition, collection and analysis, the author of this thesis intends to find out what errors the students are most likely to make in their translation practice and what causes their errors, and to provide data for translation teaching.

3.1.2 Subjects

This thesis is based on a study on an exercise of the students majoring in English at Wuhan Institute of Technology. The subjects involved in the study are 47 students from three classes in Grade 2006. These students are in their second year of undergraduate programme and in their first year of translation learning programme. These sophomores from three classes have learned basic skills and knowledge of English for one year and a half before attending the translation class. They have received the training of basic English skills, such as comprehensive English, pronunciation, listening, reading, oral English, writing, grammar. So they have mastered the knowledge of basic English grammar to a certain degree, and acquired the ability of expression and communication in listening, speaking, reading and writing in English by and large, but they haven't participated in TEM-4 nor have they attended other professional courses like British & American Literature, Linguistics, etc.

The data studied are collected from the students' translation exercises on April 10, 2008, around the middle of the semester. This translation exercise is required to be finished in a week after class. Students can look into dictionaries or any reference books. Before translating this exercise, they have done such exercises for five times, but those exercises were mainly sentences. This is the second passage they've practiced.

3.1.3 Materials

The original passage is presented in the following, with sentences numbered by the author of the paper. This passage was written by a famous American writer — John Steinbeck(1902—1968), who once won the Nobel Prize in Literature in 1962. It is the first part of his essay named *What Makes a Teacher*? In this essay Steinbeck eulogized his three teachers in plain words with full affection.

What Makes a Teacher?

[1]*It is customary for adults to forget how hard and dull and long school is.* [2]*The learning by memory of all the basic things one must know is a most incredible and unending effort.* [3]*Learning to read is probably the most difficult and revolutionary thing that happens to the human brain and if you don't believe that, watch an illiterate adult try to do it.* [4]*School is not easy and it is not for the most part very much fun, but then, if you are very lucky, you may find a real teacher.* [5] *Three real teachers in a lifetime is the very best of my luck.* [6]*My first was a science and math teacher in high school, my second, a professor of creative writing at Stanford, and my third was my friend and partner, Ed Richketts.* [7]*I have come to believe that a great teacher is a great artist and that there are as few as there are any other great artists.* [8]*It might even be the greatest of the arts since the medium is the human mind and spirit.* [9]*My three teachers had these things in common: They all loved what they were doing.* [10]*They did not tell, they catalyzed a burning desire to know.* [11]*Under their influence, the horizons sprung wide and fear went away and the unknown became knowable.* [12]*But most important of all, the truth, that dangerous stuff, became beautiful and very precious.*

3.2 Findings and Analysis

3.2.1 Findings

According to translation criteria of TEM-8, we corrected students' translation exercises. After error recognition and description, we categorized students' errors into three linguistic levels: words, phrases and sentences. Under each level, errors are also divided into several types.

The translation errors in the students' exercises we collected are listed in Table 4-7, and the frequencies of linguistic errors in students' translation are listed in Table 4-8.

Table 4-7 Linguistic errors in the translation of the students

Linguistic Category and Error Types			Examples of Error
Words	Improper translation of proper nouns	People's Name	人名 *Ed Richketts* 不译
		Place name	*Stanford* 译作"斯坦佛"
	Improper translation of common words	Wrong use of Chinese characters	真理不再是令人望而却步的东西(Original: *the truth, that dangerous stuff, became beautiful...*)
		Improper choice of corresponding Chinese words	去监管成年的文盲是怎样尝试识字的吧(Original: *watch an illiterate adult try to do it*)
Phrases	Awkward collocation		学习是一种难以置信的和没有尽头的努力(Original: *The learning... is a most incredible and unending effort*)
	Misinterpretation		在众多十分重要却暗含危机的现实情况中(Original: *the truth, that dangerous stuff, became beautiful...*)
Sentences	Misinterpretation		这也许是最伟大的、以人的意念为材料的艺术。(Original: *It might even be the greatest of the arts since the medium is the human mind and spirit.*)
	Awkward syntactic structure		成年人能忘掉沉闷、枯燥以及漫长的校园生活是一种习惯。(Original: *It is customary for adults to forget how hard and dull and long school is.*)
	Ambiguity		虽然他们并没有说出来,但却散发出一种强烈的求知的渴望。(Original: *They did not tell, they catalyzed a burning desire to know.*)
	Over-translation		三位真正的人师堪称我最好的贵人。(Original: *Three real teachers in a lifetime is the very best of my luck.*)

Table 4-8 Frequencies of linguistic errors

Students number: 47

Category	Error Types	Number of students making errors	Percentage(%)	Ranking
Words	People's Name	23	48.9	4
	Place name	6	12.8	6
	Wrong use of Chinese characters	2	4.3	9
	Improper choice of corresponding Chinese words	41	87.2	1
Phrases	Awkward phrasal collocation	29	61.7	3
	Phrasal misinterpretation	2	4.3	9
Sentences	Syntactic misinterpretation	12	25.5	5
	Awkward syntactic structure	33	70.2	2
	Ambiguity	5	10.6	7
	Over-translation	3	6.4	8

3.2.2 Error Analysis

1. Errors in choosing denotation or connotation of words

Errors of this type are the most common one, which calls for our close attention. One difficulty in choice of meaning comes from the fact that the meaning of a word is multidimensional. In their book *The Meaning of Meaning* written in 1923, C. K. Ogden and I. A. Richards present a "representative list of the main definitions which reputable students of meaning have favored" (p. 186). G. Leech in a more moderate tone recognizes seven types of meaning in his *Semantics* (p. 23), first published in 1974, as follows.

(1) Conceptual meaning: logical, cognitive, or denotative content.

(2) Connotative meaning: what is communicated by virtue of what language refers to.

(3) Social meaning: what is communicated of the social circumstances of language use.

(4) Affective meaning: what is communicated of the feelings and attitudes of the speaker/writer.

(5) Reflected meaning: what is communicated through association with another sense of the same expression.

(6) Collocative meaning: what is communicated through association with words which tend to occur in the environment of another word.

(7) Thematic meaning: what is communicated by the way in which the message is organized in terms of order and emphasis.

The average word has three component parts: sound, denotation, and connotation. Denotation is the dictionary meaning of the word; connotation is what it suggests beyond its literal meaning, its overtones of meaning, which is acquired in its past history or associations, in the circumstances in which it has been used.

Many students have difficulty in distinguishing the denotation from the connotation and are unable to choose the appropriate meaning of the words according to its specific context in translating the source text. It obviously doesn't meet the requirements presented in the Test Syllabus of TEM-8(2004) "the translation should be faithful to the source text with smooth expression and appropriate choice of words".

Here are a lot of examples. In sentence [10] "*They did not tell, they **catalyzed** a burning desire to know*", some students translate "catalyzed" into "催化". The denotative meaning of the word "catalyze" is "to make a chemical reaction quicker by adding a catalyst"(催化). After analyzing the source text and taking the context into consideration, we realize this denotative meaning is not appropriate. When we look into other connotative meanings of the word, the connotation "to cause an important change or event to happen" (导致重大变化,激发,促进) is more proper in the context.

This example shows that many students just simply choose the denotative meaning of the word to translate the original text without thinking about its context. In the following examples, some students choose the connotative meaning of the word instead of the

· 8 ·

denotative meaning; nevertheless, it's still not proper in context.

In sentence [3] "*Learning to read is probably the most difficult and revolutionary thing that happens to the human brain and if you don't believe that, watch an illiterate adult try to do it*", some students translate the word "revolutionary" into "善变". Obviously it's the connotative meaning of the word; however, the denotative meaning "变革性的" is more appropriate here. And to the word "watch", one student translates it into "监管", while we can just translate it into "看" or "好好看看".

Some translations are not faithful to the original text, because they are wrong in affective meaning. For example, "a most difficult and revolutionary thing" is translated into "一项令人费尽心机的工作". The tone of the source text is appreciative, but the diction of this student makes people feel that the author wants to express a derogatory meaning. Both these occasions are owing to their ignorance of context.

2. Failure in producing idiomatic Chinese expression

No matter whether it is awkward phrasal collocation or awkward syntactic structure, both errors are resulted from the fact that the expressions are not idiomatic. Therefore, we discuss these errors together. Since there's bound to be many differences between Chinese and English, we have to undergo what Nida calls a process of "restructuring". In doing so "the words chosen and sentences constructed must all be in such a nature as will convey accurately the real meaning of the original and at the same time conform to the usage of the target language" (1984:15). He also states that "the best translation does not sound like a translation" (1984:10). Actually, in the process of translation, the translator is not passive or totally subject to the source language text. He or she is active and creative when setting out to translate.

In the students' exercises, some expressions as "一种难以置信的和没有尽头的努力", "三位受益匪浅的老师" are mechanical translation. This kind of phrasal collocation is obviously unacceptable in Chinese. Such kind of errors also appears in sentences. The translator is too much confined by the source language, and translates the original phrases word for word. However, it is not consonant to Chinese expression. This is partially because students ignore the disparities between English and Chinese.

3. Errors in translating proper noun

The source text is written mainly in simple common words, and therefore, students wouldn't find it too hard to understand the meaning. From the error analysis, we can see that 48.9% of students have problems in translating people's names. In these students' translation exercises, they just copy the English name instead of translating it into Chinese. It is worth paying attention to. One of the possibilities is they don't know how to translate it. After all, they are beginners, and they haven't thought about how to translate it in their minds, or even to look it up in some reference books. This also reflects the translator's sloppy attitude to his or her translation. He or she has not enough sense of responsibility. What they care about is to finish the homework as quickly as possible, instead of translating it well. Another possibility is they believe that the translation of people's names is not important. Perhaps teachers also share the opinion and don't teach students proper ways to translate people's names.

In the source text, there is a place name "Stanford". Some students don't know how to translate it. For those names for specific places, the better way is to accumulate the knowledge by extensive reading. Of course, teachers should also teach students some resource books to consult.

4. Errors due to misinterpretation of sentences

A French translator once said, "Translation is understanding and being understood." For a good translation, the first step, of course, should be comprehension. Without accurate comprehension of the original version, what translators express is not exactly the original text. Thereafter, translation activities would end up in failure.

Table 4-9 Statistics of students making errors in each sentence

Students number: 47

Sentence number	Number of students making errors	Percentage(%)	Ranking
No. [1]	13	27.7%	7
No. [2]	22	46.8%	3
No. [3]	5	10.6%	8
No. [4]	25	53.2%	2
No. [5]	3	6.4%	11
No. [6]	15	31.9%	5
No. [7]	4	8.5%	10
No. [8]	26	55.3%	1
No. [9]	1	2.1%	12
No. [10]	15	31.9%	5
No. [11]	5	10.6%	8
No. [12]	16	34.0%	4

According to Table 4-9, we can see that students are most likely to make mistakes in translating sentence [8] "*It might even be the greatest of the arts since the medium is the human mind and spirit*", and their interpretations of this sentence vary. They translate it like: "在人类大脑和精神的博物馆里,优秀教师甚至可以说是最伟大的艺术家。""这也许是最伟大的、以人的意念为材料的艺术。""甚至于最伟大的艺术来自于人们的思想与精神为媒介。"This sentence is just the most difficult sentence to understand, because it is abstract and suggestive, we need to combine it with context in understanding. Translation is a transferring activity involving both the source language and the target language. The misunderstanding of the sentence directly results in errors in the sentence.

There is another representative error in sentence [12] "*the truth, that dangerous stuff, became beautiful and precious*". Many students don't recognize "that dangerous stuff" is an apposition of "the truth". They don't paraphrase this sentence correctly. As a result, their translations are ambiguous, for example, "但是最重要的是这个事实,学习这个危险的东西,变得如此美好和珍贵。""真理,往往危险事物,变得美丽和珍贵。""那些危险的通过教育之后会变得好,这是难能可贵的。" This reflects students' poor grammatical knowledge.

3.2.3 Implications

In this section, we will discuss the causes of the students' errors based on the above error analysis.

1. Lack of serious translation attitude

In some students' translations, we find that they even use Chinese characters in a wrong way. Maybe it's due to their carelessness; however, it might also result from their lack of serious attitude. Moreover, some students are only content with knowing one denotation of the word, without thinking clearly whether it is appropriate or not. They haven't thought of looking up the word in the dictionary to check out if there is any other meaning more appropriate. In students' translation practice, some choose to give up translating the complex sentence. It's also related to their lack of sense of responsibility, too.

2. Lack of context awareness

An overwhelming portion of students can't distinguish denotation from connotation and thus fail to choose the appropriate meanings of the words in translation, which shows that they are lack of context awareness. They aren't aware of the importance of contextual knowledge.

3. Lack of translation training or practice

Students' difficulty in translating proper nouns like people's names and place names, their deficiency in grammar analysis, and insensitiveness to the disparities between English and Chinese, all manifest they are lack of training in translation skills. Since they are beginners of translation learning, some of their errors can be understood. But these problems call for teachers' attention in their later teaching.

4. Poor Chinese competence

Awkward phrasal collocation, awkward syntactic structure and even wrong use of Chinese characters all reflect the translator's Chinese competence. If the translator is sensitive enough to Chinese, he or she would become more aware about the collocations of Chinese. Those awkward Chinese expressions are resulted from the weak Chinese knowledge of students. As we know, universities only offer Chinese course in the first semester in the teaching programme. Students' Chinese skills and competence are mainly acquired in their high schools. Few students make further study in Chinese in the university. Therefore, it is not surprising that wrongly written characters, wrong use of characters and ungrammatical Chinese sentences are seen here and there in their translations.

4 Suggestions for Translation Teaching

In the preceding part, we have found out some typical translation errors as well as the causes of the errors. In this part, we will focus on some relevant suggestions to translation teaching so as to help students cope with the problems.

4.1 Enhancing Translation Responsibility

In students' translation practice, some choose to give up translating the complex sentence. Certainly, it's not beneficial for their learning. Students should be told that they should have sense of responsibility. This is not only for the good of author and the reader, but also for the good of themselves. Teachers should cultivate students' good habit of doing every translation exercise well, especially as beginners. Students should be encouraged to try their best to translate and not be afraid of making errors. Teachers can help them correct errors and make improvements.

Teachers can encourage students to revise their translations several times after finishing them. During this process, they can revise some obvious errors by themselves, such as spelling, collocation problems, which is also beneficial to help them to overcome carelessness. As Newmark states, "Translation is for discussion". Students can be encouraged to discuss with their classmates how to translate somewhere better in their practice process after class to get improvement together. They don't need to be confined by some translation principles in their practice, and they only need to appreciate and assimilate the strong points of the principles. Teachers can't be available all the time, so students can discuss with other classmates, and assimilate others' strategies. During the discussion, students can realize the strong points and weak points of themselves. In this way, students can also improve their interest in translation, because interest is the best teacher for their learning.

4.2 Improving Context Awareness

British linguistist J. R. Firth once said, "Each word when used in a new context is a new word." Context plays a significant role in deciding the concrete meaning of the word in the source language. Teachers can suggest students to read more original English works in order to cultivate students' context awareness.

4.3 More Training in Translation Skills and More Instruction

Since so many students find it difficult to translate people's names, teachers should tell students some useful methods instead of ignoring the problem, and tell them some useful resources to turn to, such as transliteration form of English to Chinese （英译汉译音表）. Teachers can provide more practice exercises to students at class in dealing with proper names. With some practice, students could grasp the method of translating people's names by themselves little by little.

With regard to place name, apart from students' accumulation by themselves after class, teachers can also choose some representative place names, separate them in groups and teach students every class to enlarge their horizons. Teachers can also take this measure: first, let students collect various place names individually; later, students can share their collection in class. In this way, we can attract more students to participate in class teaching process and stimulate their interest in translation.

Most of time, misunderstanding of the sentences, especially the complicated ones, is because of their deficiency in grammar analysis. Therefore, teachers can help students overcome this problem by enforcing the exercise of complicated sentences in large numbers. This exercise can get students be accustomed to this type of complicated sentences and master some basic grammar analysis skills, so as not to be afraid of translating this type of sentences. After all, confidence is the first step of successful translation.

The students of this study are beginners of translation learning, and they have acquired few translation skills, so some of their errors can be understood. They also lack translation experience and tend to ignore the disparities between English and Chinese. Therefore, teachers can emphasize these disparities through contrastive analysis of Chinese and English and let students be familiar with the characteristics of both languages, which can decrease students' translation errors effectively.

4.4 Improving Chinese Competence

Students' exercises also reflect their deficient Chinese competence. Most English majors in China believe that since Chinese is their mother tongue, there is no need for them to learn it any more. They believe that there should not be any difficulty for them to express in Chinese what they have learnt from the source text. In their mind, the only difficulty lies in understanding the source text which may have new words and complex sentences. However, to be a qualified translator, understanding the source text is only the first step. Teachers can guide students to read extensively, such as classic works at home and abroad. To read more famous English works is to cultivate students' sensitiveness to context, while to read more Chinese classic works can help students convey the meanings of the source text in more appropriate Chinese language.

5 Conclusion

   Translation is an indispensable instrument for the communication between different countries. Its history is virtually as old as the emergence and development of language. As to English majors, translation competence even manifests the comprehensive capacity of both English and Chinese, which involves the mastery of vocabulary, grammar, and the ability of comprehension and expression of students.

   Through our error analysis of the students' English to Chinese translation, we find that they have deficiency in basic skills in both English and Chinese, and their translation competence is poor. Moreover, they are careless and content with superficial understanding. Therefore, in the process of translation teaching, it's necessary for teachers to assist students with effective teaching of translation methods and help them get rid of bad habits of translation. Teachers can provide more practice exercises for students at class and tell them several basic principles as well as some reference books. To students' misunderstanding of complicated sentences, teachers can help students overcome this problem by enforcing the exercise of complicated sentences in large numbers, and emphasize these two languages' disparities through contrastive analysis of Chinese and English. Students should be encouraged to try their best to translate and not be afraid of making errors. Teachers can encourage students to check their translations several times after finishing them, suggest students to read more original English works in order to cultivate students' consciousness sensitivity to context and suggest students read extensively both English and Chinese.

   It might be impossible for the students to do a perfect job in translation in a short time, especially at the beginning, but the most important thing is to make students feel that translation process is full of interest and satisfaction.

Bibliography

[1] CORDER S P. Error analysis and interlanguage[M]. Oxford: Oxford University Press, 1981.

[2] BROWN H D. Principles of language learning and teaching[M]. Beijing: Foreign Language Teaching and Research Press, 2001.

[3] JEAN D, HANNELORE L-J, CORMIER M C. Translation terminology[M]. Beijing: Foreign Language Teaching and Research Press, 2004.

[4] NEWMARK P. A textbook of translation[M]. Shanghai: Shanghai Foreign Language Education Press, 2001.

[5] NIDA E A. Language structure and translation[M]. London: Longman, 1984.

[6] NIDA E A. Language, culture and translating[M]. Shanghai: Shanghai Foreign Language Education Press, 1993.

[7] Pearson Education Limited. Longman Dictionary of Contemporary English[M]. Beijing: Foreign language Teaching and Research Press, 2000.

[8] 董任. 英语修辞学概论[M]. 上海：上海外语教育出版社, 1999.

[9] 杜广华. 对比分析法、错误分析法和语际语理论间的关系[J]. 山西农业大学学报, 1997.

[10] 翻译理论与翻译技巧论文集[M]. 北京：中国对外翻译出版公司, 1985.

[11] 方梦之. 翻译新论与实践[M]. 青岛：青岛出版社, 2004.

[12] 穆雷. 中国翻译教学研究[M]. 上海：上海外语教育出版社, 1999.

[13] 高校外语教学指导委员会英语组. 高等学校英语专业英语教学大纲[S]. 上海：上海外语教育出版社, 2000.

[14] 胡壮麟. 语言学教程[M]. 北京：北京大学出版社, 2001.

[15] 华先发, 邵毅. 新编大学英译汉教程[M]. 上海：上海外语教育出版社, 2004.

[16] 蒋红红. 剖析翻译实践中的问题译文现象[J]. 南华大学学报, 2007(8).

[17] 刘宓庆. 新编当代翻译理论[M]. 北京：中国对外翻译出版公司, 2005(10).

[18] 刘重德. 文学翻译十讲[M]. 北京：中国对外翻译出版公司, 1990.

[19] 刘靖之. 翻译论集[M]. 香港：三联书店, 1981.

[20] 上海外国语大学四、八级考试命题研究组. 2008英语专业8级考试翻译指南[M]. 青岛：中国海洋出版社, 2007.

[21] 申雨平. 西方翻译理论精选[M]. 北京：外语教学与研究出版社, 2002.

[22] 温秀颖. 英语翻译教程[M]. 天津：南开大学出版社, 2001.

[23] 杨士焯. 从一篇翻译看英语专业三年级学生的翻译问题[J]. 中国翻译, 2000.

[24] 杨士焯. 英语专业三年级学生如何提高英汉翻译技能[J]. 中国翻译, 2002(11).

[25] 张春芳. 中国翻译教学初探[D]. 上海：上海外国语大学，2004.
[26] 钟慧连. 从汉译英错误分析看英语本科翻译教学[D]. 桂林：广西师范大学，2004.

Appendix

英译汉参考译文

为师之道

  成年人往往忘了当年上学多艰苦、多乏味、日子多漫长。为了把那些基本的东西背诵下来,花费的力气实在是无穷无尽,让人难以置信。识字读书也许是人的脑子碰上的最艰巨、变革性最大的事情。如果不信,看一看成年的文盲是怎样尝试识字的吧。上学不是件轻松的事,大部分时光也没有什么趣味;不过,要是你的造化好,也许会碰上位真正的老师。我最大的幸运,就是一生中有过三位真正的老师。第一位是中学里教理化和数学的老师,第二位是斯坦福大学里教写作的教授,第三位就是我的朋友、合作者——埃德·雷克茨。

  如今我相信一位良师就是一名大艺术家,而且良师就像任何其他大艺术家一样地难得。教书甚至可以说是一门最伟大的艺术,因为这门艺术传播的是人的思想和精神。

  我的三位良师有如下共同之处:他们全都热爱自己的工作;他们并不灌输知识,而是激发学生求知的热望。在他们的影响下,我的眼界豁然开朗,忧虑消失了,未知变成了可知。可最为重要的是,我们所寻求的真知,不再是令人望而却步的东西,而是变得美好而珍贵了。

(张秀明译,选自《英语世界》1992年第5期)

4.4　A Thesis on Linguistics

The Influence of Thematic Progression on Coherence in College English Writing

Abstract

English writing is not only a very complicated course, but also one of the language skills most difficult to improve. College English compositions are full of many problems, and incoherence is one of them. The coherence of an English text depends not only on the cohesion of grammar and lexis, but also the coherence in meaning. According to textual linguistics, thematic progression is an important factor to ensure the coherence of a text. As to the relationship between thematic progression and coherence, many scholars from home and abroad have done a lot of research. However, most of these researches just stay at the stage of applying thematic progression in analyzing coherence of the paragraph, and the research of applying thematic progression in analyzing coherence of the whole text has not been carried out much. Based on this cognition, the thesis attempts to apply thematic progression in analyzing the coherence of the whole text.

The thesis gives a clear idea of thematic progression first, and then it analyzes coherence of examples of the college students' English writings by applying thematic progression. Finally the thesis proves that both writing coherence and writing ability of students can be improved by fostering their textual consciousness through the theory of thematic progression.

Key words: thematic progression, coherence, college students' English writing

摘 要

作为最重要的语言能力之一,写作近年来在大学英语教学中受到越来越多的关注。英语写作是一个非常复杂的过程,也是较难提高的语言技能之一。大学英语作文写作中普遍存在许多问题,而文章缺乏连贯性便是问题之一。英语语篇的连贯与否不仅体现在语法和词汇的衔接上,而且还体现在语义的连贯上。主位推进是保证语篇语义连贯的重要因素之一,关于主位推进与连贯的关系,国内外许多学者已进行了大量的探讨和研究,但大多数都停留在应用主位推进分析段落的连贯性这一层次上,而应用主位推进分析整个篇章的连贯性这一层次的研究却很少进行。基于这一发现,本文将尝试应用主位推进对整个篇章的连贯性进行分析。

本文首先详细地介绍了主位推进模式,然后使用主位推进来分析大学生英语写作实例的连贯性,最后证明了在大学英语写作教学中,如果注重运用主位推进理论来培养学生的语篇意识,学生写作的连贯性和写作水平均会得到提高。

关键词:主位推进,连贯,大学生英语写作

Contents

Abstract ·· (I)

摘要 ·· (II)

1　Introduction ··· (1)

2　Literature Review ·· (3)

　2.1　Review of Thematic Progression Research ··· (3)

　2.2　Danes' Patterns of Thematic Progression ··· (4)

　　2.2.1　Simple Linear Thematic Progression ··· (4)

　　2.2.2　Thematic Progression with a Constant/Continuous Theme ············· (5)

　　2.2.3　The Derived Pattern ··· (6)

　2.3　Thematic Progression and Coherence ··· (8)

3　Studies on College English Writing ··· (9)

　3.1　Problems in College Students' English Writing ······································· (9)

　3.2　Guidance Function of Thematic Progression in College English Writing ········· (10)

　3.3　The Application of Thematic Progression in College English Writing ····· (10)

　　3.3.1　The Application of Thematic Progression in a Paragraph ··············· (11)

　　3.3.2　The Application of Thematic Progression to a Whole Text ············ (13)

4　Conclusion ··· (21)

Bibliography ··· (22)

1 Introduction

In College English Test (CET), writing is a kind of test means which embodies student's English level, and it is also one of the language skills most difficult to improve. A lot of university students can already write out compositions that accord with grammar rules but give people a vague and non-smooth feeling in organization of the text, expression of the idea and arrangement of the structure. Aiming at the problems existing in students' English writing, a lot of experts and scholars have made untiring efforts, and have carried out analysis and research on students' English compositions from different angles, and one of the important aspects is to apply the theory of textual linguistics to the research on the problems of textual cohesion and coherence rather than general grammar mistakes in English writing.

How to effectively use cohesive devices to improve English writing has been a hot topic of foreign language teaching research in recent years. There have been a lot of correlative achievements. Some scholars think that cohesion, which is necessary in text building, correlates with the quality of student's compositions to some extent. In English writing, many Chinese students use few textual cohesive devices, and this makes their compositions unsmooth and the sentences shift from one topic to another abruptly. This fact relates to the lack of cohesive sense. Besides, the applications of cohesive devices in Chinese students' English writing and native foreigners' writing have distinct differences: Chinese students use much fewer cohesive words and phrases than English native speakers. In addition, even those Chinese students who have rather good English skills in lexical and grammar, have such problems in their writings, such as ambiguous references, misuse or overuse of conjunctions, ambiguity of demonstrative pronouns, and a limited use in lexical cohesion and so on (Beaugrande & Dressler, 2001; Witte & Faigley, 2002; 杜金榜, 2001; 徐伟成, 2000). Some other scholars apply the cohesive theory of Halliday and Hasan (2001) to describe and analyze the application actuality of cohesive devices in Chinese college students' English writing. At the same time, they bring forward some opinions about how to train students' abilities to apply various cohesive devices so as to strengthen textual coherence (陈香, 2002). These researches from home and abroad indicate cohesion, that endows the words with textual property, is the basis of textual coherence, and can be useful in organizing the textual structure.

From above studies, it can be seen that these scholars just try their best to roundly describe the usages of different cohesive devices in English writing, but don't excogitate an effective model to direct teachers and students to analyze the text in English writing class so as to intensify the teaching and learning effects in English writing class. Focusing on this aspect, this thesis attempts to apply an effective way "thematic progression" that can analyze coherence in English writing to help students realize that in a text each sentence always has regular relations with other sentences. When it comes to the concept of "thematic progression", two important terms should be mentioned, that is "theme" and "rheme", which were firstly brought forward by the founder of the Prague School, V. Mathesius(黄国文,1998). Since then, many linguists have done many studies in such a field as Halliday's expatiation on "theme" and "rheme" (Halliday, 2000). Moreover, "thematic progression" is a theory put forward by Frantisek Danes(黄国文,1998). It mainly includes three patterns of thematic progression by Danes' early proposal. The appearance of thematic structure and thematic progression has opened a new field for language study. These theories have great practical value. Some language educators have tried to apply thematic structure and thematic progression patterns in foreign language teaching; and some of them have already made preliminary achievements. Based on these achievements, linguists began to make research on thematic progression and coherence. However, up to now, most studies are just staying at the level of applying thematic progression to analyze coherence of a paragraph, and the study of analyzing coherence of a whole passage has not been carried out much.

Therefore, based on the theories of researchers from home and abroad, this thesis intends to deal with coherence of the whole text from thematic point of view, and to illustrate thematic progression as a major contributor to coherence of the whole text. Besides, the thesis, in applying thematic progression in analysis of college students' English compositions, tries to find out the textual incoherence and to revise these incoherent compositions, thus providing implications for both teachers and students in future English writing.

2 Literature Review

2.1 Review of Thematic Progression Research

Theme and rheme are the two terms which were first put forward by the founder of Prague School, Vitem Mathesius in 1939. He analyzed how information is distributed in sentences to make a text coherent. Each simple sentence has a theme "the starting point of the utterance" and a rheme, everything else that follows in the sentence which consists of "what the speaker states about, or in regard to, the starting of utterance" (Mathesius, 1942). Later Halliday and some other linguists accepted the terminologies of theme and rheme. According to Halliday, the role of theme serves as a point of departure of a message, often reflecting the topic of utterance; and the rest, the part in which the theme is developed is the rheme. That is, the known information is regarded as the "theme", and the new information the "rheme". Here is an example.

① *John sat in the front seat.* ② *In the front seat sat John.*

John is the grammatical subject in both sentences, but theme in ① and rheme in ②.

To further illustrate the theme and rheme structure, the following Table 4-10 gives an example.

Table 4-10　Theme-Rheme Structure

Theme	Rheme
The duke	has given my aunt that teapot.
My aunt	has been given that teapot by the duke.
That teapot	the duke has given to my aunt.

Though Halliday (2000) stresses the function of themes in organizing a text by stating that the choice of themes plays a fundamental part in the way discourse is organized, and this in fact constitutes what is often known as the "method of development of the text". In theory, Halliday himself has not elucidated thematic progression. The study is made mainly by Fries and Danes.

Danes' contribution is to extend the concept of theme as point of departure of a single utterance (sentence) to that of explaining the texture of text. His basic assumption is, "the choice and ordering of utterance themes, their mutual concatenation and hierarchy, as well as their relation to the hyper themes of the superior text unit, such as the paragraph, chapter..., to the whole text, and to the situation. Thematic progression might be viewed as the skeleton of the plot." (Danes, 1974:114). Danes suggests a number of ways in which strings, chains, themes and rhemes may interact in text (1974:118-119).

Every sentence has its own theme and rheme. When a sentence exists alone and has no context, its theme and rheme are fixed. However, most texts are constructed on the basis of more than two sentences which are internally related. Thus the theme and rheme in the following sentences will have some connection with the theme and rheme in the former sentences. The connection between sentences is realized with the progression process from theme to rheme. This is called thematic progression.

In his book *Zur Linguistschen Analyse des Textstrukfer*, Danes points out that the essence of thematic structure lies in the cohesion and coherence of the themes in the clause, their internal relationship and their relationship with the content and the text. He claims that the progression from theme to rheme represents the basic structure of a text. As theme is the starting point of a message, thematic progression in paragraphs is closely related to the writer's purpose of writing. Danes thinks that from the point of text organization, it is the theme that plays an important constructing role.

The thematic organization of the text is closely connected with how discourse is connected. The discourse and its paragraphs can be regarded as the succession of themes. In a coherent discourse, sentences are not freely grouped together and there is a certain law guiding the train of thought. While people are creating a text, they connect the inner-related sentences together to express a complicated idea. The real thematic progression of a discourse actually refers to the cohesion and connection of the themes, the relationships between themes and their subordinates and the relationship between themes, the paragraph, the whole discourse and the setting. All these kinds of relationships can be thought as "the pattern of thematic progression".

2.2 Danes' Patterns of Thematic Progression

After much observation of different types of texts, Danes (1974) points out that there are some rules in the arrangement of thematic structures, and therefore he comes up with three main types of thematic progression patterns: simple linear thematic progression, thematic progression with a constant/continuous theme and thematic progression with the derived pattern.

2.2.1 Simple Linear Thematic Progression

Danes (1974: 118) refers to this pattern as the most elementary or basic thematic progression. In this pattern, the rheme or a part of the rheme in the preceding clause becomes the theme of the subsequent clause. The following example and graph (see Fig. 4-6) manifests this model (T=theme; R=rheme).

The first Europeans (T1) to set foot in Texas were Spanish explorers (R1). For

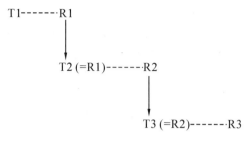

Fig. 4-6

many years the Spaniards (T2=R1) *who colonized Mexico heard stories of "the Great Kingdom of the Tejas"* (R2). *These stories* (T3=R2) *described Native American people* (R3).

In this text, the theme of the first sentence is *The first Europeans*; the rheme of the first sentence *Spanish explorers* is taken up as theme of the second sentence *Spaniards*. And the rheme of the second sentence *stories of "the Great Kingdom of the Tejas"* becomes the theme of the third sentence *these stories*.

In this pattern, each theme naturally grows out of each previous rheme, and the whole paragraph is coherent as themes are clearly related. As the theme develops, new content is presented to the reader one after another. It is easier for the reader to get the main train of the writer's ideas. The writer will usually employ this thematic pattern to describe or explain the object to the reader, or to emphasize the theme or rheme. An example from CET-4 (College English Test Band 4) can also illustrate this pattern clearly.

Nowadays, if you want to seek employment (T1), *mostly you will have to go through a job interview before you can get it* (R1). *A job interview* (T2=R1) *enables both the interviewer and the interviewee to get a fairly clear picture of each other* (R2).

2.2.2　Thematic Progression with a Constant/Continuous Theme

The theme in the preceding clause is employed as the themes in the subsequent clauses, which is illustrated as follows (see Fig. 4-7).

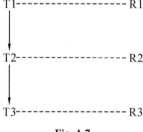

Fig. 4-7

Peter H. Fries called this type of thematic progression theme iteration. Here, the same theme enters into relation with a number of different rhemes. The result of this type of thematic progression is that the themes in the text constitute a chain of co-referential items, which extends through as sequence of sentences or clauses. Rhemes describe the different aspects of the same event or thing from different angles. Here is an example.

The saw-scaled viper (T1) is found in dry sandy areas where there is little vegetation (R1). Its length (T2) is about two feet (R2), and it (T3) is sandy in color with darker spots (R3). It (T4) is aggressive and very poisonous (R4). It (T5) may be found in the full blaze of the sun or beneath hot stones and in crannies heated by the sun (R5).

This text is taken from a booklet on survival in tropical forests, and it provides an illustration of constant thematic progression (TP) pattern in use. The theme of each clause refers wholly (it) or partially (its length) to the main topic of the text, the saw-scaled viper (Bloor T, Bloor M, 2001: 90).

With regard to Chinese college students' English writing, this pattern is also commonly used in the compositions of CET-4. Here goes one example from some model writings of CET-4.

Yet many others (T1) don't think so (R1). They (T2) think that numbers have nothing to do with luck (R2). They (T3) regard numbers simply as mathematic symbols for counting. They are anything but a mystery (R3). They (T4) laugh at those who think numbers can bring good luck (R4).

2.2.3 The Derived Pattern

1. The derived themes pattern

The first clause is the topic sentence; the themes in the subsequent clause may derive from the theme of the first clause. The diagram (see Fig. 4-8) below can be used to show this clearly.

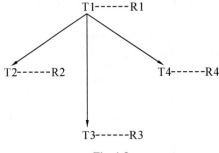

Fig. 4-8

In this type, the theme of the first clause is often called hypertheme of the text. The themes of other clauses are all derived from this so-called hypertheme. Theme and rheme expand separately at the same time. Here is an example.

Thousands of people (T1) rush into big cities every year (R1). Some (T2) come for education (R2). Some (T3) come for shopping or sightseeing (R3). Some (T4) come on business (R4).

Each of the subordinate themes here is derived from the hypertheme "thousands of people". This kind of thematic progression pattern is normally used as the beginning paragraph of students' compositions, particularly argumentations. The following example from CET-4 illustrates this point.

Different people (T1) *have different opinions about money* (R1). *Some* (T2) *hold that money is the source of happiness* (R2). *In contrast*, *other people* (T3) *think that money is the root of all evils* (R3).

2. The derived rhemes pattern (The split rheme pattern)

Another point to emphasize is a type of thematic progression pattern, which is denominated as the split rheme pattern by Danes (1974). However, recently it is commonly categorized into the type of the derived progression by linguists, such as Huang Guowen (1998).

The themes in the subsequent clauses may derive from the rheme of the first clause. It can be represented diagrammatically as follows(see Fig. 4-9).

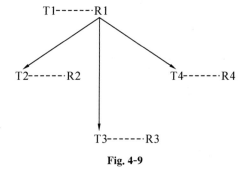

Fig. 4-9

The following is an example.

For a long time, *humans* (T1) *have caused* a number of pollutions (R1). The first type of pollution (T2) *occurs in the water where marine lives have been destroyed by oil spills and illegal dumping* (R2). The second type of pollution (T3) *happens when humans contaminate the land with landfills or the use of pesticides to treat their lawns or crops* (R3). *And* the worst (T4) *is the air pollution with the ever increasing number of automobiles which emits carbonmonoxide into the air* (R4).

The first sentence has a rheme "a number of pollutions". In the following three sentences, each one illustrates a kind of pollutions. Moreover, each applies one kind of pollutions as its theme, which is derived from the original rheme of the first sentence.

This kind of thematic progression pattern is frequently used to illustrate a certain point in compositions, which is widely adopted in argumentations in CET-4 as follows.

Being honest (T1) *will benefit not only others*, *but also ourselves* (R1). *First* (T2), *your honesty will make others willing to trust you* (R2). *Second* (T3), *being honest can lead you to face your problem bravely*, *which helps to solve it* (R3). *And* the last (T4), *honesty surely helps to make the society more harmonious* (R4).

2.3 Thematic Progression and Coherence

The means of realizing textual cohesion consist of grammatical cohesion, lexical cohesion and thematic cohesion. Thematic cohesion interacting with grammatical and lexical cohesion enhances the cohesion of the text and its internal organic information organization. The thematic organization of the text is closely connected with discourse coherence or text connection. A text is defined as text largely in terms of its semantic coherence; however, it is useful to remember, as Danes (1974) points out that texts are not always perfect; they not only display coherence to an uneven degree, but some may be characterized as "discontinuous". Textual coherence, in this light, is not a yes-or-no property but rather a more-or-less property. Normally, different patterns of thematic progression correlate with different types, but most texts have complex patterns of thematic progression, i.e., they do not have one single strategy. Thematic progression is one of the most important theories of discourse coherence, and it is one of the effective ways for exploring the structure of an article (黄国文, 1998: 73). Thematic progression analyzes discourse coherence from the inside of the discourse. And thematic progression reflects the way of thinking of human beings.

To summarize, the thematic progression helps to create textual coherence in that it structures the clause so that the clause is more likely to succeed in conveying the intended message on the part of the writer, and interpretation is facilitated and oriented on the part of the reader.

Generally speaking, seen from the point of view of thematic progression, both a good English writing and the model-writing from CET-4 cohere well. Therefore, in the following part, more examples will be provided to illustrate the functions of thematic progression.

3 Studies on College English Writing

3.1 Problems in College Students' English Writing

Writing effective texts, whether in native language or foreign language, involves many different areas of knowledge and skills. These include the ability to generate suitable content, and to organize the content coherently; the ability to form syntactically correct sentences, and to link them to form coherent text; and the knowledge of a sufficiently wide range of vocabulary and syntactic patterns to express a variety of concepts. All these make enormous demand on a writer.

A common complaint of teachers in college is that their students fail to develop their ideas when asked to write a composition. The students may have a lot of relevant ideas and a considerable number of basic facts about the subject, but they don't know how to organize these ideas to produce a coherent article. Lack of cohesion in writing is a problem that plagues students. One type of cohesive devices is always overused. For example, the same words are used repeatedly in their writings. Lacking a large vocabulary, linguistic knowledge and skills in constructing English texts, students often keep shifting the topics from one to another, leaving the reader an impression of discontinuity of coherence.

There must be some causes responsible for the occurrence of the problems. One of the main causes is the writer's thought pattern. Westerners consider subject and object, material and spirit diametrically, i. e. , things just have two possibilities, either this or that. When thinking, westerners usually start from parts, and then think about the whole situation, which is called "linear thinking mode". Easterners are used to making a compressive survey of the overall situation first, and then thinking over details. They depend on intuition and are imbued with imagination. People call this "round thinking mode". The process of writing is the right process of organizing different ideas and concepts into something perceivable and tangible for the purpose of communication. The writing of different cultures will reflect their thought pattern differences. Chinese students tend to think in Chinese and transfer meanings of their native language to the English language by using Chinese writing strategies. So how to help students overcome the problems has long been a challenge to both teachers and researchers.

3.2 Guidance Function of Thematic Progression in College English Writing

Why can't students improve their English writing level even though they have studied English for many years? Reasons of this question are certainly in many aspects. But for my part, that our traditional writing teaching seems to overly pay attention to the permutation association of English sentences is one of them. In fact, more attention should be paid to the connection between sentences in paragraph, and English writing teaching methods should be improved. If teachers can analyze the rule of thematic progression in the process of teaching English writing, there is no doubt that they can improve students' awareness of the text as a whole. At the same time, teachers can apply the model of thematic progression in the analysis of college English writing model essay and students' compositions, and in order to strengthen students' awareness of coherence, teachers should also analyze the compositions' advantages and disadvantages in terms of coherence of the whole text according to the theory of theme-rheme and thematic progression.

3.3 The Application of Thematic Progression in College English Writing

While correcting college students' compositions, teachers usually find that some compositions are grammatically correct and good in word choice, but lacking in fluency and smoothness. These compositions are awkward to read, because the whole texts or some parts are unsmooth and the sentences often shift from one theme to another abruptly. Therefore the thesis attempts to apply "thematic progression" in analyzing and commenting on students' English compositions.

In addition, one good composition should show high degree of textual coherence besides few mistakes and correct structures of sentences. That is, no sentence is completely isolated, and each sentence should be related to the preceding and following sentences, just as the British linguist Fries points out, "... each sentence should follow logically from what has done before. This implies in part that the point of departure of each sentence should relate in some way to what has preceded. If there are unexplained jumps in the sentence of starting point, that implies that there breaks in the argument" (Fries, 1995: 121). A good composition shouldn't have any such "break", but on the contrary, in inferior compositions "breaks" occur frequently.

In the following study, all the examples are cited from Chinese college students' English compositions. These compositions represent typically a number of common problems. Through detailed analysis, some most common and serious problems existing in college English writings can be found out.

3.3.1 The Application of Thematic Progression in a Paragraph

The following paragraph is from *Chinese Learners English Corpus*.

Example 1

The computer (T1)// *is a great invention of this century. The invention* (T2)// *has greatly changed our ways of working and living ever since the first computer came into the world. A lot of things* (T3)// *would become impossible without computers. The world* (T4)//*would not be what it is today.*

Through careful analysis, it can be seen that the problem lies in the improper thematic progression pattern. As mentioned in 2.3, the means of realizing the textual cohesion consist of grammatical cohesion, lexical cohesion and thematic cohesion. Thematic cohesion interacting with grammatical and lexical cohesion enhances the cohesion of the text and its internal organic information organization. The whole paragraph needs to be organized through the gradual progression from known information (*The computer*) to new information (*The invention*) and from new known information (*The invention*) to another new information (*our ways of working and living*). By adjusting the themes and rhemes, the paragraph can be revised as the following.

Example 1' (revised)

The computer (T1)// *is a great invention of this century. Ever since the first computer came into the world,* (T2) *this invention has greatly changed our ways of working and living. Without computers,* (T3)// *a lot of things would become impossible and the world would not be what it is today.*

The revised version mainly adopts the constant theme pattern. The known information falls on the same theme, and the thematic progression encourages the information flow from known (*The computer*) to new (*invention*) and to another new (*our ways of working and living*). The whole paragraph is much more coherent than the first version.

The procedure of thematic progression can be illustrated as follows (see Fig. 4-10 and Fig. 4-11, the asterisk * stands for "theme break").

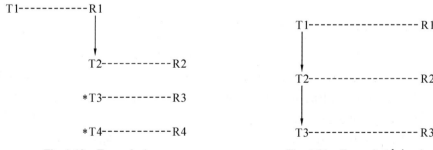

Fig. 4-10　Example 1　　　　　　　　Fig. 4-11　Example 1' (revised)

· 11 ·

By comparing these two diagrams, it can be seen that two theme-breaks occur in the original version, that is T3 and T4, because these two themes have no relation to the themes of the preceding sentences while there is no theme breaks in the revision. The paragraph develops its theme according to the constant theme pattern.

Another paragraph is selected from one student's composition as follows.

Example 2

Trees (T1) are man's friends (R1). We (T2) can see trees (R2) everywhere. We (T3) plant trees (R3) every year. We (T4) can make tables (R4) with trees. Trees (T5) also give us fruits (R5) to eat. I (T6) like to eat fruits (R6) very much.

By analyzing the paragraph carefully, it can be found that the writer used some cohesive devices such as the recurrence of words (trees) and conjunctions (so). But the whole paragraph doesn't express a definite central idea. Therefore, this paragraph just achieves grammatical cohesion, but doesn't achieve semantic coherence. Thus, taking the textual cohesion and coherence into account, the paragraph can be revised as follows.

Example 2' (revised)

Trees (T1) are man's friends (R1). They (T2) provide man with timber, fruits and seeds (R2). With timber (T3), man can build houses and make furniture (R3). Fruits (T4) are the food, which is necessary to us everyday (R4). As for seeds (T5), they can be used to extract oil (R5).

The following diagrams (see Fig. 4-12 and Fig. 4-13) can be used to show the procedure of thematic progression.

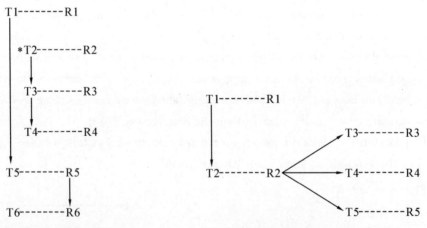

Fig. 4-12 Example 2   Fig. 4-13 Example 2' (revised)

From the diagram it can be seen in the original version there is semantic relation between T1 and T5, R5 and R6; however, although T2, T3, and T4 are the same, they don't have necessary coherence with sentence 1 and sentence 5. That is, there is one theme break (T2) in the original version. However, the revised version adopts the constant theme pattern and the derived rhemes pattern. Sentence 1 is the topic sentence of the whole paragraph. The following sentences are the developing sentences of the topic. Thereby, focusing on the topic "Trees are man's friends", the whole paragraph achieves semantic coherence.

3.3.2 The Application of Thematic Progression to a Whole Text

Up to now, many scholars have done a lot of researches on the application of thematic progression in paragraph, but the study on the application of thematic progression in a whole text has not been carried out much. Thereby this thesis attempts to apply thematic progression in analyzing the whole text.

The following composition is chosen from the descriptive writing task completed by one of my partners (Wang Fang, College of Material, Grade Four, Class One).

Example 3

My Dormitory

① *I (T1) live in Room 401 of the No. 2 building.* ② *This (T2) is a comfortable room.* ③ *Four girls (T3) are in this room, and they are very kind.* ④ *I (T4) love them very much.* ⑤ *My bed (T5) is above my desk, and it is very big.* ⑥ *Beside the bed (T6) is my wardrobe.* ⑦ *There are so many clothes (T7) in it.* ⑧ *We (T8) have a big balcony.* ⑨ *It (T9) has so much sunshine, because it faces south.* ⑩ *We (T10) plant many flowers on the balcony, so it looks very beautiful.* ⑪ *Standing on the balcony (T11), we can see the lawn.* ⑫ *It (T12) looks like a green sea.* ⑬ *Every dorm (T13) is similar.* ⑭ *Opposite my dorm (T14) is boy's dormitory.* ⑮ *We friends (T15) are very kind.* ⑯ *They (T16) usually help me, and I usually help them, too.* ⑰ *Our dorm (T17) is very clean.* ⑱ *I (T18) love my dorm very much.*

Reading this text, we may get an impression that there are not many problems with its single sentence, but it seems to be not coherent enough, for new information just keep emerging abruptly at the beginning of some sentences. For instance, the first two sentences are a general introduction of her dorm, whereas the third sentence begins with a definitely new information "Four girls" as its theme. After a continuous description about the relationship between the author and her roommates, abruptly enough, another new information turns up as the theme of the fifth sentence—"my bed". The following sentences introducing the layout of her dormitory don't have such "theme jumping" problems, until the last two sentences of this text. Sentence 13 "Every dorm is similar", the emergence of which is so unexpected that it gives readers a weird feeling; and sentence 14 "opposite my dorm is boy's dormitory", the coherence problem of which lies in two aspects: one is that it has deviated from its central topic "my dormitory"; another is that it has nothing to do with the sentence preceding it. Later on, the author jumps suddenly to describe her roommates and the relationship between them once again.

It seems that without awareness of coherence in the mind, the author just jotted down

· 13 ·

whatever popped into her mind, never considering whether the preceding sentence is coherent with the following one or not. Despite of some deficiencies, the author did apply certain thematic progression patterns in the description of the layout of her dorm, though in an unobvious way. For example, the thematic progression pattern of sentence 5 and sentence 6 is constant theme pattern, and the thematic progression pattern of sentence 10 and sentence 11 is simple linear theme pattern. This may suggest that there exists certain thematic progression patterns in our subconscious mind, though not in a systematized way.

A diagram (see Fig. 4-14) can also be drawn to show its procedure of thematic progression as follows.

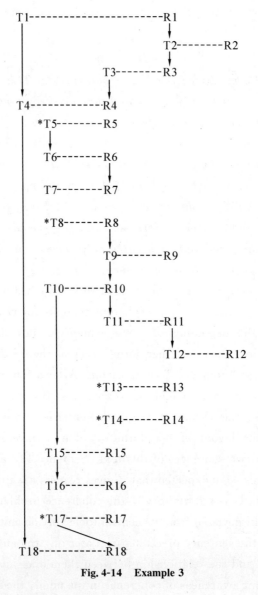

Fig. 4-14 Example 3

From the diagram it can be seen that there are five theme breaks (T5, T8, T13, T14 and T17) in the original version. The whole text doesn't cohere well.

Gaining some knowledge on thematic progression after my patient explanation, Wang Fang revises this composition according to the model of thematic progression. The passage below is Wang Fang's second version.

Example 3' (revised)

My dormitory

① *I (T1) live in Room 401, Building No. 2.* ② *It (T2) is a comfortable room where lives four girls.* ③ *They (T3) are very kind and usually help me.* ④ *I (T4) love them very much.*

⑤ *The room (T5) faces south and has many beautiful flowers.* ⑥ *It (T6) isn't a big room, but it's bright and clean.* ⑦ *In the room (T7), there are four desks, wardrobes, and chairs.* ⑧ *My desk (T8) is very clean.* ⑨ *My wardrobe (T9) has many clothes.* ⑩ *Beside the wardrobe (T10) is a window.* ⑪ *From the window (T11) we can see a lawn, which looks like a green sea.* ⑫ *There (T12) plant many trees.* ⑬ *They (T13) look very beautiful.*

⑭ *I (T14) live happily in my dorm and I love it very much.*

Firstly, in this revised version, the author groups information of different registers into three different paragraphs. The first paragraph is a general introduction of her dorm and the relationship between her and her roommates; the second is about the layout of the dorm; and the third expresses her affection towards her dorm.

Secondly, when checking the writing from the aspect of the application of the thematic progression patterns, we find that the degree of coherence has been greatly improved. There is almost no abrupt emergence of themes. In the first paragraph, the author generally applies the simple linear theme pattern; and in the second paragraph, she begins with the constant theme pattern and turns to the simple linear theme pattern in describing the layout. The whole text focuses on the theme "I" and/or rheme "room". The selection of patterns of thematic progression contributes a lot to the coherence of the whole text.

Thirdly, due to the removement of the redundant information from the third paragraph and the application of the constant theme patterns, the revised third paragraph is neat and more coherent with the whole text.

The following diagram(see Fig. 4-15) can help clearly show the procedure of thematic progression for the revised example.

From the diagram it can be seen that the revised version mainly apply the simple linear theme pattern and the constant theme pattern, and there is no theme break in the whole text. Each sentence has some relation to the preceding sentences, showing high degree of textual coherence.

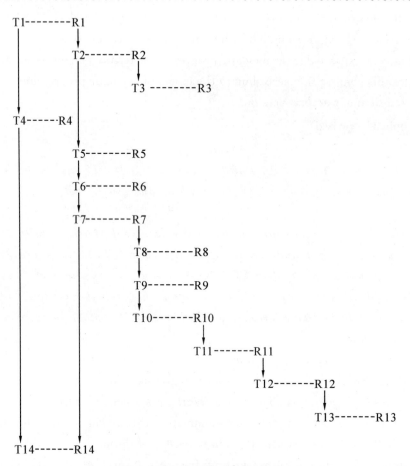

Fig. 4-15 Example 3' (revised)

Here goes another composition from the argumentative writing task completed by another partner of mine (Meng Yan, College of Environment, Grade Four, Class Two).

Example 4

① *First of all, let's* (T1) *have a clear picture of the general conditions of China's education.* ② *Now, China* (T2) *still has very low level of education.* ③ *Compared with a large population of students, schools* (T3) *are not enough in China.* ④ *Students* (T4) *can be provided with more chances to receive education by private schools.* ⑤ *Secondly, the country's heavy burden* (T5) *can be relieved by private schools.* ⑥ *Different from public schools, private schools* (T6) *are supported by individuals.* ⑦ *Therefore the country* (T7) *doesn't take the responsibility of giving the financial support to these private schools.* ⑧ *Furthermore, the taxes paid by the private schools* (T8) *can do good to the country.* ⑨ *Money gained from these private schools* (T9) *can be put in developing our country's education.*

This text elaborates the advantages of encouraging private schools in China. The writer gives several reasons supporting the idea. In spite of the fact that in the text there does exist some grammatical and lexical cohesive devices, such as the cohesive words "first of all", "now", "secondly", "therefore", "furthermore", the text still doesn't cohere well. Though the basic patterns of thematic progression are embodied in the text, when examining the themes listed above, we can see that the themes are rather confusing. For example, the theme in the second sentence is "China"; in the third sentence is "school"; and in the fourth and fifth sentences, the themes are "students" and "the country's heavy burden". Thus, it lacks logical connection between these themes, which results in the confusion in structure and vagueness in meaning and consequently affects the coherence of the composition.

A diagram(see Fig. 4-16) can be used to show the procedure of thematic progression for this example.

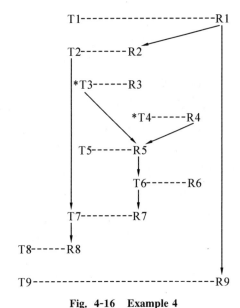

Fig. 4-16 Example 4

This diagram shows there are two theme breaks in the original version, and themes of the whole text are very dispersive, causing textual incoherence.

The following is a revised version written by the present author.

Example 4' (revised)

① *Let's (T1) have a clear picture of the general conditions of China's education.* ② *First of all, China's education level (T2) is still so low that schools are insufficient in China compared with a large population of students.* ③ *Private schools (T3) can provide students with more chances to receive education.* ④ *Secondly, private schools (T4) can relieve the country's heavy burden.* ⑤ *Different from public schools, private schools (T5) are supported by individuals.* ⑥ *Therefore the country (T6) doesn't take the responsibility of giving the financial support to these private schools.* ⑦ *Furthermore the country (T7) can benefit from the taxes paid by the private schools.* ⑧ *Money gained*

· 17 ·

from these private schools (T8) *can be put in developing our country's education.*

The procedure of thematic progression is illustrated as follows(see Fig. 4-17).

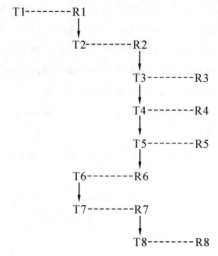

Fig. 4-17 Example 4' (revised)

From the example, it can be noticed that by revising only some of the themes according to the theories of thematic progression, without changing the content of the text, the meanings of the passage are much clearer. The whole text develops its themes mainly according to the simple linear theme pattern and the constant theme pattern.

Peter Fries claims that the content expressed by thematic progression patterns should sketch the structure of a text (Fries, 1995). A clear structure can inevitably help to enhance the coherence of a text. In the revised version, "private schools" has been used four times as the theme. These successive themes make the text compact and the logical meaning closely related, thus generating coherence in the deeper level of the writings.

One more example comes from the present author. This composition was written in 2006 when the present author was in Grade Two in college. The title of this composition is "The Importance of Teamwork".

Example 5

The Importance of Teamwork

①*In fact, teamwork* (T1) *has proved to be meaningful both for society and for personal life.* ②*Selfishness* (T2) *can be left behind because people can care for others and society better through teamwork cooperation.* ③*Many shortcomings* (T3) *brought by individuals are also overcome or avoided so that a great efficiency is obtained.* ④*The teamwork* (T4) *will also help people to get to know each other better and love each other better, which will greatly help the whole society get more closely united and lived.* ⑤*At the same time the teamwork* (T5) *will make collectives more and more powerful and a nation stronger and stronger, which will substantially reduce the criminal rate or terrorism.* ⑥*In the coming years, we* (T6) *should also cooperate with other nations to be* successful in the world economy as the development of economic globalization. ⑦*Obviously teamwork (T7) is also very important in a worldwide project and very useful for the creation and maintenance of a peaceful world environment.*

After reading the whole text, we find there is no grammatical mistakes on the whole, and the rough meaning is also clear, that is, teamwork is meaningful both for society and for personal life. This text has some textual linking markers such as "also, at the same time". But after careful analysis, it is easy for readers to find the whole text lacks coherence.

While maintaining the content of the original version, the present author revises the whole text as follows.

Example 5' (revised)

The Importance of Teamwork

① *In fact, teamwork (T1) has proved to be meaningful both for society and for personal life.* ② *Through teamwork cooperation (T2), people can care for others and society better, leaving selfishness behind.* ③ *During the cooperation (T3), people can learn a lot from one another and many shortcomings brought by individuals are also overcome or avoided so that a great efficiency is obtained.* ④ *Teamwork (T4) will also help people get to know each other better and love each other better, which will greatly help the whole society get more closely united and lived.* ⑤ *At the same time, teamwork (T5) will make collectives more and more powerful and a nation stronger and stronger, which will substantially reduce the criminal rate or terrorism.* ⑥ *In the coming years, global market and competition (T6) will surely have greater requirements for international cooperation.* ⑦ *So teamwork (T7) is also very important in a worldwide project and very useful for the creation and maintenance of a peaceful world environment.*

The following diagrams (see Fig. 4-18 and Fig. 4-19) can show the procedure of thematic progression clearly.

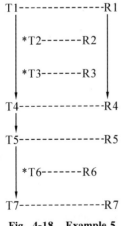

Fig. 4-18   Example 5

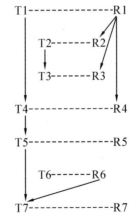

Fig. 4-19   Example 5' (revised)

From the diagram it can be found in the original version that T1, T4, T5, and T7 continue naturally and they are ultimately the same. However, T2 and T3, R2 and R3, T6 and R6 have no relation to the preceding and subsequent themes. That is, there are three theme breaks in this text (T2, T3, and T6). These sentences often make readers feel very abrupt. Obviously, the whole text lacks coherence.

Although the revision is not perfect enough, the procedure of thematic progression is clearer. The whole text mainly applies the constant theme pattern, and each sentence is linked up to the preceding and subsequent sentences. So the whole text gets more coherent.

4 Conclusion

Based on the theories of researchers from home and abroad, this thesis has analyzed textual coherence of college students' English compositions by applying thematic progression. From the analysis above, a conclusion can be drawn that thematic progression is a very important instrument to achieve the textual coherence although it is not the only approach. The research on thematic progression facilitates displaying the essence of textual coherence. Choice of the patterns of thematic progression correctly plays a decisive role in constructing smooth, natural texts. At the same time, the analysis of the model of thematic progression helps reveal the author's writing purpose, and enables the readers grasp the skeleton of the article and know the developing direction of the article as soon as possible. Teachers can apply the theory of thematic progression from the textual level in the process of writing teaching so that more coherence can be achieved in the students' writing.

College English writing in China has long been considered as the weakest skills of students. English writing is a big headache to teachers and students. Therefore, it is a critical task to probe into the new teaching method. By applying the model of thematic progression in the English writing teaching timely, and making it not only stay at the theory level, but also exert the function of guiding practice, the present study will certainly produce a far-reaching influence on both teaching and learning of English writing.

Of course, there are several limitations of the present study. It is maybe not all-inclusive and the conclusion is tentative since only two types of writing are analyzed and the total number of examples is not sufficient. Further studies can be carried out to apply the thematic progression in the teaching and learning of English writing of college students at different English levels.

Bibliography

[1] BEAUGRANDE R, DRESSLER W U. Introduction to text linguistics[M]. Beijing: Foreign language Teaching and Research Press, 2001.

[2] BLOOR T, BLOOR M. The functional analysis of english: a Hallidayan approach[M]. Beijing: Foreign Language Teaching and Research Press & A Hodder Anorld Publication, 2001.

[3] DANES F. Papers on functional sentence perspective[M]. Prague: Academia, 1974.

[4] GHADESSY M. Thematic development in English texts[M]. London: Pinter, 1995.

[5] HALLIDAY M A K, HASAN R. Cohesion in English[M]. Beijing: Foreign language Teaching and Research Press, 2001.

[6] HALLIDAY M A K. An introduction to functional grammar[M]. Beijing: Foreign language Teaching and Research Press, 2000.

[7] QUIRK R, GREENBAUM S, LEECH G, SVARTVIK J, et al. A comprehensive grammar of English language[M]. London: Longman, 1942.

[8] WITTE S, FAIGLEY L. Coherence, cohesion, and writing quality[M]. Beijing: Foreign language Teaching and Research Press, 2002.

[9] 陈香. 语篇的连贯性与大学英语写作[J]. 零陵学院学报, 2002(4).

[10] 杜金榜. 从学生英语写作错误看写作教学[J]. 外语教学, 2001(2).

[11] 胡壮麟. 语篇的衔接与连贯[M]. 上海: 上海外语教育出版社, 1994.

[12] 黄国文. 语篇分析概要[M]. 长沙: 湖南教育出版社, 1998.

[13] 马静. 主位推进、语义衔接与英语写作的连贯性[J]. 外语教学, 2001(5).

[14] 徐盛桓. 主位和述位[J]. 外语教学与研究, 1982(1).

[15] 徐盛桓. 再论主位和述位[J]. 外语教学与研究, 1985(4).

[16] 徐伟成. 英语作文中的衔接、连贯与质量[J]. 广州大学学报, 2000(5).

[17] 张育红. 主位推进与写作的连贯性[J]. 国外外语教学, 2004(2): 47.

[18] 朱永生. 主位推进模式与语篇分析[J]. 外语教学与研究, 1995(3).

参 考 文 献

[1] DEVLIN B. 英语论文写作教程——基于国际标准的学术写作与发表[M]. 北京:清华大学出版社,2007.
[2] SEYFER H,吴古华. 英语学术论文写作[M]. 北京:高等教育出版社,1998.
[3] ROSEN L J,BEHRENS L. Writing papers in college[M]. Boston:Little, Brown and Company,2000.
[4] GIBALDI J. MLA 科研论文写作规范[M]. 上海:上海外语教育出版社,2001.
[5] FABB N,DURANT A. How to write essays, dissertations and theses in literary studies[M]. 成都:四川大学出版社,2003.
[6] 丁往道,吴冰. 英语写作手册[M]. 北京:外语教学与研究出版社,1994.
[7] 高等学校外语专业教学指导委员会英语组. 高等学校英语专业英语教学大纲[M]. 北京:外语教学与研究出版社,2000.
[8] 黄国文,葛达西,张美芳. 英语学术论文写作[M]. 重庆:重庆大学出版社,2007.
[9] 教育部高等教育司. 高等学校毕业设计(论文)指导手册[M]. 北京:高等教育出版社,2001.
[10] 李正栓. 英语专业本科毕业论文设计与写作指导[M]. 北京:北京大学出版社,2006.
[11] 刘涛波,李如平,袁蕾. 大学英语论文写作手册[M]. 重庆:重庆大学出版社,2006.
[12] 牟杨,陈春莲. 英语专业毕业论文写作指南[M]. 武汉:武汉大学出版社,2007.
[13] 石坚,帅培天. 英语论文写作[M]. 成都:四川人民出版社,2007.
[14] 田贵森,段晓英. 英语专业毕业论文写作教程[M]. 北京:北京理工大学出版社,2006.
[15] 文秋芳,俞洪亮,周维杰. 应用语言学研究方法与论文写作[M]. 北京:外语教学与研究出版社,2004.
[16] 张纪英. 英语专业毕业论文写作教程[M]. 武汉:华中科技大学出版社,2007.
[17] 张秀国. 英语专业毕业论文写作教程[M]. 北京:清华大学出版社,北京交通大学出版社,2007.
[18] 周开鑫. 英语专业学生学术论文写作手册[M]. 北京:外语教学与研究出版社,2006.